CONTEMPLATION

400 Questions for the Inquisitive

GEORGE STYLES, Ph.D.

No part of this book may be reproduced, or stored in a retrieval system, or transmitted in any form or by any means, electronic, mechanical, photocopying, recording, or otherwise, without permission of the author or publisher.

Copyright © 2021 George Styles

All rights reserved.

Cover Design: George Styles

Cover Illustration: © Vian Peshdary

ISBN: 9798469702689

CONTENTS

PREFACE   1

SECTION 1: QUESTIONS   4

SECTION 2: INSIGHTS   44

ACKNOWLEDGMENTS   264

PREFACE

The aim of *Contemplation* is not to give any definitive answers, nor is it to point the reader towards what the author may think is the correct answer. Rather, the questions, the insights, and the references are intended to give the reader a clarification and a head start. Rarely, a given insight may contain two references or more, but generally, references are intended to start the reader off on one possible direction of thought. As many of the questions, if not all, may not have any real answer, this pursuit is left up to the reader to decide for themselves. Hence, the questions are numbered and listed in the 1st section of the book, and further info is listed in the 2nd "Insights" section of the book for that same listing. I have purposely made the two sections separate in case the reader wishes to examine a question without seeing any insights. This, in case one wishes not to have their thoughts immediately influenced. The questions deal with life, psychology, and science, but also a number of open-ended questions that may be in various genres and fields. The idea behind the questions is that they may, in fact, be unanswerable at this present time. However, with some thinking and perhaps some research from interested parties, perhaps there may be definitive answers for many, if not all, of these queries. The insights are my own clarifications of the intent that I had in mind while formulating the questions. This is not to be taken as the only way to think about the questions but rather as a spark that lights a bonfire. Also, the reader is quite right to take their own direction with the questions and insights and mentally branch off from any of the insights I have provided. It is hoped that the reader will also question and challenge the insights so as to find new views on them. This, as it is often that new and valuable insights come from attempting to see things from a different angle. Most especially, new ideas and views always seem to come from questioning things. In terms of the references I have provided, these are only published academic or dictionary sources. Any other types of citations are unverifiable and hence, not suitable sources.

GS

SECTION 1: QUESTIONS

1. Is most of attraction superficial?

2. In research, how do you suppose researchers might consider something more or less 'figured out?'

3. Do you ever consider how old the ideas are behind your beliefs, and/or does this matter at all to you?

4. Do you think people would get way further ahead if they admitted their weaknesses and vulnerabilities to themselves instead of pretending they don't have any?

5. Is laziness the cause of most, if not all, of humanity's problems?

6. Is atheism a religion?

7. Do you know love when you see it?

8. Other than adverse events, how does one gain humility?

9. What behavior would make you break up with someone on the spot?

10. Do you truly believe that people can change within their lifetime?

11. If, time after time, people keep falling for the same tricks, what, in your opinion, does that say about H. sapiens?

12. Are you suspicious of those who push to seek advancement in jobs?

13. Do you consider yourself to be confident?

14. Why are we pushed, perhaps way too much for our own good, in childhood, to make and have friends?

15. What can't be disputed?

16. What, in theory, can't be tested?

17. If you never had to work again, would you?

18. If you could go back to school for anything right now, what would it be?

19. What is the difference between religion and philosophy?

20. Why are some people convinced that what they "feel" is right and that logic doesn't matter?

21. Can you name a negative consequence of escapism?

22. Are you suspicious of people that seem to like to only point out your faults or shortcomings?

23. Are video games healthy?

24. Why are there no holidays where we go out and visit science museums and such things?

25. Do you think in the future, using genetic biotechnology, that they will attempt to create real life werewolves and vampires?

26. Can you fix 'stupid?'

27. What are the downsides to a world that has no "common sense?"

28. Why do people legitimize those who deny facts/truth?

29. Can you personally prove that there is no objective reality?

30. Are all ideas original, or is there always some degree of overlap with pre-established ideas?

31. Are humans able to conceive of all possible concepts?

32. Is "smart" an illusion?

33. Does true, 100% security exist?

34. Does a person get smarter in proportion to the number of books they read, courses they take, plus experiences they engage in?

35. Overall, what do you think humans are destined for?

36. Have you ever examined why you think the way you do?

37. Innate notions aside, where do most of your personal ideas come from?

38. Are systems and rankings of people just collective illusions within our intersubjective consciousness?

39. Is there a cure for jealousy?

40. Why do people tie so much of others people's value to employment?

41. Why are "bad guys" so revered?

42. Why are certain people popular, and others are not?

43. Why is it that you try to help some people, and they take your kindness as either idiocy or weakness?

44. Why do so many people only think something is an issue if it's in the news?

45. Do you think that there are people who don't fall for any deception?

46. What is the difference between a legit theory and a conspiracy theory?

47. Do humans have their own existence figured out?

48. What could be wrong with a start date for the universe/existence/world being 4004 BC?

49. How long do you think it will be till wheel-less hover cars are the norm?

50. What are the symptoms of being surrounded by toxic people?

51. What is your personal policy about dealing with/interacting with edgy, need-to-walk-on-egg-shells-when-around sort of folk?

52. What should science know more about?

53. Do you question rules?

54. Why are people convinced that they absolutely must have beliefs?

55. If squirrels and other animals wrote and read books, do you think so many would end up as roadkill?

56. Will your legacy have an impact on future generations?

57. What might it imply when it is said that humans never learn from history?

58. What are some falsehoods that the human brain can perpetuate?

59. Is it a common trait for humans to enjoy thinking?

60. Where do most people get their notions and concepts from?

61. Are people "their actions?"

62. If alien life was found to be heading to earth within the next month, what would you do?

63. Do you consider yourself someone who has no problem questioning authority?

64. Can you go through life without judging anyone?

65. Will humankind be done with the supernatural within the next 100 years?

66. Why do people come up with conspiracy theories?

67. Do you believe in 'luck?'

68. Did you take more or less risks after you were married with kids?

69. What do you hate being questioned?

70. Do you think biology explains all of human behavior?

71. Do impossibilities truly exist?

72. In the case of people that don't get along, is it that they can't get along or won't get along?

73. Do you think it's possible that if we work together and stick together, that we could build heaven right here on earth?

74. If I am designed to sin, why would I be punished and have to repent?

75. What has you convinced there is an afterlife?

76. Do you think, given our current state, that we could slip into a second round of dark ages?

77. Do you believe animals have the sense to foresee major natural disasters or weather phenomena?

78. Do you backup or confirm your personal knowledge with research?

79. Do you consider yourself robust to the power of mass influence?

80. Do you think plants have sentience?

81. Despite the benefits alleged, is it possible that exercise can also be a negative for health?

82. If everyone has an opinion that is equal to all other opinions, then why do most people only trust/run to very few and very select folk for an opinion when it comes to something critical?

83. What do you believe in with full certainty?

84. Do you ever look up a word to see when it first appeared according to linguistic scholars?

85. Where, anatomically, do things like thoughts, beliefs, emotions and perceptions exactly sit in the brain?

86. What is the difference between the quantum interpretation from Heisenberg and Bohr (Copenhagen Interpretation)... and the quantum interpretation of David Bohm?

87. What is one clue that something is a definite scam?

88. What should we not be straightforward about?

89. What is the trickiest part of life to get through?

90. Do you think the Machiavellian way is a good approach to dealing with people?

91. How many people in a democracy, do you think, actually understand/know how a democracy ACTUALLY works?

92. Are you someone who can shrug anything off, or are you the complete opposite of this?

93. Is all you have truly yours?

94. If you literally don't care, is this believing?

95. Can you name something that can be perfectly neither proven or disproven by science?

96. Have you ever met someone who did a lot of stuff in life, but didn't seem to take much, if anything, from all of it?

97. Do you think there are people who think that freedom means "I can be as nasty to others as I want to be?"

98. What is the worst emotion to experience?

99. Do you find you tend to meet or exceed expectations or disappoint the people you know?

100. Would you consider yourself a leader or a follower?

101. Do humans like dogs more than they like other humans?

102. Do you think what people will and won't spend money on could be considered revealing of their true character?

103. If you had a Wikipedia page about you, how long do you think the article would be?

104. Do we really need people to rule us?

105. Do you think that there are any historical figures that didn't exist?

106. Can you, with confidence, tell the difference between an anthropocentric point of view or idea from one that is not?

107. Can it be perfectly proven beyond a shred of a doubt that there are absolutely NO FACTS?

108. Do you think that it is imperative that people should have at least one hobby?

109. If it affects you, is it your business?

110. Would you rather face or ignore reality?

111. Can you ever be too determined?

112. Does the universe really care about us?

113. If someone wrongly but badly humiliates you, do you just let it go?

114. Why does disease exist?

115. Did you ever have any friends that just wanted to be told only what they wanted to hear?

116. Guardian Angels: Do they exist?

117. Have you ever had a young/mid/old or any other sort of life crisis?

118. How far into the future do you envision your plans, goals and dreams?

119. Do you find that people tend to overcomplicate things?

120. Why do you suppose people praise others for their stance rather than their content?

121. Is craving attention or needing praise and/or clout a behavioral thing, an addiction, or a pathology?

122. What is it about the word 'evidence' that scares so many people?

123. Do you think that the 'modern' world, although having definite positives, is a bit more than humans are evolved to handle?

124. The human sense of shame: Have we lost it, or was it always a rare bird?

125. How far back do you know your family history?

126. Do you believe that only things that have been tested by science can be considered as fact?

127. What do you think would happen if inheritance was abolished?

128. What do you consider a power trip?

129. What things do some people race to cry victim over, but are actually all their own fault?

130. What started the trend of accusations becoming convictions?

131. IYI = Idiot Yet Intellectual. What do you consider an IYI?

132. How did entitlement start?

133. Do you think there really is a difference between generations?

134. Professionals snooping Social Media accounts... Is this professional behavior by professional people?

135. Do you think a newly confirmed nihilist is someone who has figured it all out, or someone who is but a mere rookie with philosophy?

136. What do you owe people?

137. If someone who lacks empathy is a psychopath, then what is someone who lacks self-reflection?

138. Do you think it is somehow possible to avoid 'growing up?'

139. Are "armchair experts" a source of disinformation?

140. Would you say that you are just like everyone else?

141. Does ego have any benefits?

142. Are there more 'bona fide' experts in the world, or more armchair experts in the world?

143. Is social media simply a tool, or something that should come with a warning label?

144. If in our society 'brainwashing' is a common thing, would you know how you were brainwashed?

145. Are your friends somehow a reflection of you?

146. Why did the universe have to add consciousness to itself?

147. Do you believe that you have an eye for talent?

148. Do you know why colors exist?

149. If you had to choose, would you rather be 'tired' or 'bored?'

150. What's something you don't believe in that most people believe in?

151. Do you think the system that you currently live in is as close to perfect as it can be? Or can you imagine something better?

152. If you had to guess, do you think that consciousness is more of a set, definite program, or a set of parallel conditions?

153. Would you rather have been born knowing everything there is to know?

154. Do you think you have good celebrity potential?

155. Are you for, or against, playing it safe in life?

156. How would someone know if they were a deep person or a shallow person?

157. Why do humans need leisure?

158. Have you ever been written off after doing something well or extraordinary with someone saying "Yeah sure, I could do that too if I wanted...?"

159. Why, over time, have our names come to have less and less meaning within them?

160. Who is the funniest person you know, whether they are a celebrity or not?

161. Given that change is supposedly the only constant in the universe, what in your

opinion is the slowest thing in the universe?

162. Would you consider yourself competent at being able to tell if you are getting pulled into something that is neither in your best interest nor is your concern?

163. Space is expanding... But what is it expanding into?

164. Can you name something that is faster than light?

165. If we live and experience different realities, then why does gravity pull us all down in the exact same way?

166. Is having a solid grasp of reality in a way, a 'privilege?'

167. Are you able to tell if someone is just telling you what you want to hear as opposed to talking to you straight?

168. Have you ever asked yourself why you believe what you believe?

169. We all likely know an "Energy Vampire" or more. But exactly what is it that makes them this way?

170. Do you think a person can avoid facing 'the truths' for an entire lifetime?

171. Do you know what is meant by the saying "Having skin in the game?"

172. What would be your advice to someone who is entitled, but doesn't know any better, and finds themselves not getting anywhere in life?

173. What are some things that people hate to admit and will steer away from at any cost?

174. What is 'light?'

175. Do you trust that medications are always prescribed in your best interests?

176. Now that you've lived a good chunk of life, how much do you believe in good school grades?

177. Why do humans "worship?"

178. What is the best 'state of mind' to go through life with?

179. Do you think that unemployment will forever be a problem with the human race?

180. Do you think the following is a 'word-trick,' or does it symbolize a bona fide trait of reality? "*Nothing is still something.*"

181. In your opinion, what is the greatest set-back one can experience in life?

182. Have you ever been bored with life?

183. In any story/book, in your opinion, what are the two most important things that it absolutely must have?

184. Do you believe that "good things come to those who wait?"

185. Which people in my life, whether I know them or not, love them or not, are most likely to hold me back from my goals in life?

186. Would you say that you have high-expectations for a significant other in a relationship?

187. Are you able to sit and think beyond the average level of thoughts?

188. Do you think you would be able to tell if you were going crazy?

189. Why does the human race always end up enabling and empowering tyrants?

190. How much of what you want is really what you want... ...and how much of what you want came from external subliminal programming?

191. How many people consider themselves brainwashed at least some extent, even if it's tiny... and how many people consider themselves truly free?

192. Is creativity learned or innate?

193. Besides time and the three spatial dimensions, do you think there are other dimensions we can't immediately see 'right in front of us?'

194. What innovations do you think will come from time crystals?

195. What would you do if you lived in the time of a "Mad" Monarch?

196. Why do humans do war?

197. Do people really believe there are no set-in-stone answers to anything, or is this just a subliminal way to avoid conflict?

198. Is it sound theoretical planning and intuition or serendipity that is responsible for many scientific discoveries?

199. Since we got a number of takes on what an 'alpha-male' is, then what would a 'beta-male' be, in your opinion?

200. If you were the world's richest person, would you do it all differently than Jeff Bezos?

201. Why is the deadliest animal, deadly?

202. Have you ever considered trying out to be a secret agent?

203. Do you find it intriguing that there are many trees on earth which are older than your direct genetic lineage?

204. Is it that people need to 'think outside the box,' or 'live outside the box?'

205. Are you a personality that everyone can get along with?

206. Have you ever had an addiction that you were able to get out of?

207. Do you think it's possible that anyone could fall victim to Munchausen syndrome?

208. Many cultures, independent of one another, have built pyramids. Why pyramids?

209. Do you know what the difference between old engine oil (I.e., needs to be changed) and new engine oil is?

210. Can we say that overthinkers are more prone to anxiety and panic attacks?

211. Is evolution/change ALWAYS good?

212. Do you think we have actually 'lost' technology secrets, that might put us ahead even now, from history's empires and times now long past?

213. Were you born a 'traveler,' or did you become one as you grew up?

214. What do you think is the origin and original reason our species adorns itself with makeup, body modifications, and jewelry?

215. For those affected: Have you ever reasoned with yourself about why you get imposter syndrome?

216. Can we agree there is a sort of evolutionary sixth sense emerging in some of us that rings the bell and raises the flag when in the proximity to predatorial types?

217. Is reality TV beneficial, or does it have no effect, or is it detrimental?

218. Should anyone else have a say over your body?

219. Is it healthy to have regrets?

220. Has money made the human experience better or worse or otherwise?

221. What was the greatest scam ever?

222. Can you say you understand the concepts of 'signal' and 'noise?'

223. Is our system made the way the elites want it, or is it the way the greater populace wants it?

224. Did the internet change people, or just reveal who we really are?

225. What is more advantageous, being a deep thinker, or being an overthinker?

226. Do you think that 'Zombies' are possible?

227. Do you think it is possible to make an animal biology textbook/course about human behavior that is accurate?

228. Are you able to force yourself to get along with someone who you definitely don't get along with?

229. Can all conspiracy theories be completely written off?

230. Have humans figured anything out at all?

231. In an afterlife, would you be the same age as you were at the time of death?

232. Does meditation work?

233. What is time?

234. Do you think self-made people are really so self-made, given the interconnectedness of our society?

235. Do you believe in charity donation?

236. What do you consider to be true 'intelligence?'

237. Do you consider yourself a graduate of the school of 'hard knocks?'

238. What do you think made people choose a major religion over any alternatives?

239. Why is Jesus not written about with expected volume and respect in contemporaneous Roman texts?

240. In observing quantum mechanical experiments, do you think its possible the observer observing these experiments might be leading to misleading experimental results?

241. When you make a guess or a call on something, how often do you find that you are correct?

242. Is someone who takes regular selfies highly probable to be a narcissist?

243. Do you believe someone can be overeducated?

244. What, to you, defines a true victim?

245. Do you believe we came from a primordial muck supplemented with asteroid collsions?

246. Has there ever been anyone with true, tested and verified psychic powers?

247. Do you believe that what goes around comes around?

248. Do you ever think they will be able to perfectly unfry an egg?

249. Do you consider yourself streetsmart or booksmart?

250. Do you ever think you could have been started off on the wrong advice?

251. Do dreams come from pieces of real life, or from somewhere else?

252. Would you rather be educated or entertained?

253. Have you ever been surrounded by frenemies?

254. Is it interest or ability that determines one's true capacity?

255. Could life have no meaning?

256. Do all religions and spiritualities worship the same deity?

257. Can people accurately assess their own intelligence?

258. How many people do you think are currently affected by social anxiety?

259. Which animals besides humans are religious?

260. How much corruption actually goes on?

261. Why do humans find what they find terrifying, terrifying?

262. Is filial piety always the best path?

263. Are humans best suited for individualism, tribalism, or collectivism?

264. Is the hard problem of consciousness actually 'hard?'

265. Is there an afterlife?

266. Why are monsters scary just by appearance alone?

267. Do all questions have a correct answer?

268. Is being good at school equivalent to intelligence?

269. What started anti-intellectualism?

270. Should political correctness be made law?

271. Will marriage come to an end soon?

272. What gets in your way the most in life?

273. How much of your life was purely decided on your own ideas and terms?

274. Do you think you have ever been in the presence of a potential serial killer?

275. Do you think you are misunderstood?

276. How will quantum computers change things?

277. Why can't most people, right now, outrun Usain Bolt?

278. What will be the next species of the *homo* genus?

279. How do you know that you can be certain on a given statement or topic?

280. How long did it take for you to believe in yourself?

281. Why do humans like games?

282. Have you ever tried to invent something?

283. Why do scam artists still exist?

284. Why do people like averages and first place winners?

285. Do you think it is possible that each day we wake up into a new dimensional reality?

286. Is someone that is able to make a lot of friends a talented person?

287. Has humanity become too materialistic?

288. How do you think traffic jams affect people's mental health?

289. Do memory puzzles actually increase/enhance memory?

290. Why are lifeforms composed of cells?

291. How much of life is actually fun?

292. Do you think you can manifest your wishes?

293. Given we are highly social creatures, is it cruel to ostracize or leave out other human beings?

294. Is humanity's biggest creation the human population?

295. Have you ever felt that you were not alone in a house or a room?

296. Will we ever be able to time travel?

297. How much perception bias does the average person have?

298. Are we a naturally civil species, or are we just acting that way?

299. How long until the Amazon rainforest is gone?

300. Do you know what the difference is between physics and metaphysics?

301. In your experience, what is the ultimate illusion in life?

302. Have we seen evolution happen?

303. Do you think everyone is entitled to a home of their own?

304. Are you skeptical of things that have big hype behind them?

305. Do you think Shakespeare wrote all his own works?

306. Would you consider getting cryogenically frozen in order to be preserved?

307. Why do we experience pain?

308. How many humans can live on earth without an issue?

309. Are you in favor of a universal basic income?

310. Do people really 'fake sick?'

311. Are all humans curious?

312. Are innocent bystanders truly 'innocent?'

313. Why do people masquerade the exception as the rule?

314. If holy books are complete and comprehensive texts, then why do they not have quantum mechanics clearly outlined and included in the content?

315. Do you think if you had the opportunity and had of put your mind to it that you could have been the best at anything you wanted to?

316. Why do some parts of the world get rain and some don't?

317. What do you think needs to be reinvented?

318. What is the best solution to the world garbage problems?

319. Would you rather be born with talent, or work your way into becoming skilled?

320. Have you ever known someone who was utterly and totally unfit for a job, but was hellbent on getting it through whatever means (cheating on tests, bootlicking, nepotism, cronyism, etc) that was necessary?

321. What, in your opinion, is a 'brilliant' person?

322. Do you think that there could be some eras or periods of history that might have been all made up?

323. Do you believe that enough bad times are sure to yield some good ones?

324. Is competitiveness overrated?

325. Do you believe that governments are actually hiding evidence of UFOs?

326. Is a person's experience of love controllable?

327. As a guesstimated percentage, what do you think the overall prevalence of insecurity amongst the collective of humanity currently is?

328. Before the events that actually started Christmas, how do you think people celebrated the day that became known as Christmas way before it became what it is now known for? ...and why?

329. Are you someone who can do rollercoaster and "spinning-type" rides without becoming dizzy, nauseous, and discombobulated?

330. Do you ever think we'll make bionic organs that last longer than we do?

331. Is artificial intelligence a blessing or a curse?

332. Are some people simply greedy by their nature?

333. Do deities need to follow logic to exist?

334. Where and when did the idea of the soul come from?

335. Why do all animals and even bacteria run on glucose?

336. Is going with the flow always the best strategy?

337. Is social superiority/inferiority hardwired in the human brain?

338. Should we sequence the DNA of museum specimens of extinct animals?

339. Do you have what it takes to complete an Arctic or Antarctic expedition?

340. Do things like cells or transistors add up to become something more?

341. Is it possible that a population could become too dense and therefore affect human social behavior?

342. How long do you think a closed, self-contained colony on Mars would last?

343. Are you accountable for your own actions?

344. Do you believe that objects can be possessed/haunted?

345. How would you give an AI motivation?

346. For those of you concerned with climate change, how well do you understand the five mass extinction events?

347. Are we all equal in potential?

348. What is the future for power generation?

349. Do you think working from home should be a regular thing from now on?

350. Why can't we bring people back from the dead?

351. Could we be getting spied on?

352. How many of the world's problems are due to not being united?

353. Is kindness a normal behavior?

354. How often do you think anger is used as a distraction?

355. Do you think that we will ever fully map out the universe in terms of elementary particles and the forces between them?

356. Do you think String Theory will eventually lead to figuring out the universe?

357. Why can't we live forever?

358. When did humans begin to take stories and/or narratives as beliefs?

359. Are people generally clear on where to place blame?

360. Have different generations experienced different childhoods?

361. Will our freedoms increase as the world population increases?

362. Is modern science run in the best way possible?

363. Would you rather one single world government?

364. Do you think the world could exist without police?

365. What is the percentage of fraudulent scientific publications?

366. Is social media bad for mental health?

367. Do you think most people can admit when they are wrong?

368. What is life?

369. Can Marxism work?

370. Physical, mental or emotional, do you consider yourself a fighter?

371. Why is science denial and flat-earth theory so popular?

372. Do narcissists prefer Twitter or Facebook?

373. Why does Facebook stay afloat?

374. What is the evolutionary basis for bullying?

375. Why do people get tattoos?

376. Why do people join groups?

377. Do animals have personalities?

378. Is there such a thing as the true self?

379. Does astrology actually work?

380. Do people need ideology?

381. Do you know how an internal combustion engine works?

382. Do you understand Einstein's Special Theory of Relativity?

383. What is an intellectual?

384. Why has it become fashionable to shun obvious intelligence and verifiable knowledge?

385. What determines how your life goes?

386. Is favoritism the major driver behind advancement in workplaces and organizations?

387. Does Cancel Culture actually exist?

388. What is the point of middlemen in the business world?

389. How many people could be real psychopaths?

390. What do you think is the cause of existential crisis being so common?

391. Do you wish to leave a legacy?

392. Do I actually know what I really want?

393. In general, what is the thing you would say that people talk about the most?

394. Is time real?

395. How does time work, exactly?

396. Are time and space apart from the human mind?

397. Why do humans form beliefs?

398. Are you familiar with 'Occam's Razor?'

399. How will the universe end?

400. What happened before the Big Bang?

SECTION 2: INSIGHTS

1. Is most of attraction superficial?

INSIGHTS: Is how someone looks the primary determinant in attraction? In terms of the human sense of smell, dissimilarity between two people in a protein complex called the "Human Leukocyte Antigen" (HLA) in humans may determine a perfect match. However, on the biochemical/physiological level, attraction is also thought to have many processes and variables at work.

Kromer, J., Hummel, T., Pietrowski, D., Giani, A. S., Sauter, J., Ehninger, G., ... & Croy, I. (2016). Influence of HLA on human partnership and sexual satisfaction. *Scientific reports, 6*(1), 1-6.

Robinson, C. (2021). The Biochemistry of Attraction. *Journal of Student Research at Indiana University East, 3*(1), 126-139.

2. In research, how do you suppose researchers might consider something more or less 'figured out?'

INSIGHTS: Can we say we are finished when we deciphered all possible aspects of a given area of science? Have we explored all there is to explore within that topic? Are we finished once we can't seem to find another angle on what is being studied? When do researchers know when we are done with a given topic?

Kools, F. R., Mirali, S., Holst-Bernal, S., Nijhof, S. L., Cavalli, G., & Grandner, M. A. (2018). Publications are not the finish line: focusing on societal rather than publication impact. Frontiers in medicine, 5, 314.

3. Do you ever consider how old the ideas are behind your beliefs, and/or does this matter at all to you?

INSIGHTS: An interesting example of this is the topic of human consciousness. Although there are piles and piles of psychology, neurology, and neuroscience studies and discoveries in the literature, many of the world's people still follow an idea on consciousness from 400 AD. Since this is the case, it could mean that additional information is being missed simply because people believe the whole debate has been closed since 400 AD!

Kauffman, S., & Radin, D. (2021). Is Brain-Mind Quantum? A theory and supporting evidence. arXiv preprint arXiv:2101.01538.

4. Do you think people would get way further ahead if they admitted their weaknesses and vulnerabilities to themselves instead of pretending they don't have any?

INSIGHTS: Is it so easy to go through life without admitting one's own shortcomings and vulnerabilities? Does putting this all off make life easier? Or by putting it off, are we setting ourselves up for a disappointment down the line when we really don't need it?

Zhang, J. W., Chen, S., & Tomova Shakur, T. K. (2020). From me to you: Self-compassion predicts acceptance of own and others' imperfections. Personality and Social Psychology Bulletin, 46(2), 228-242.

5. Is laziness the cause of most, if not all, of humanity's problems?

INSIGHTS: It may not be the cause of most of humanity's problems, or is it? Are people putting in an effort for a reason, or are they just going with whatever pops up? Are humans always active in their choices and decisions, or does it just appear that way?

Pennycook, G., & Rand, D. G. (2019). Lazy, not biased: Susceptibility to partisan fake

news is better explained by lack of reasoning than by motivated reasoning. Cognition, 188, 39-50.

6. Is atheism a religion?

INSIGHTS: Many theists are quick to assume that one has to be a believer in something, but the atheist's stance is that they are the state of non-belief. Although this doesn't sit well with some theists (and predictably so), the atheist's stance is that they do not believe God exists and thus have no religion. Again, theists maintain that atheists are a religion, but atheists claim they have none of the characteristics of one and thus, are not.

Martin, M. (1992). Atheism: A philosophical justification. Temple University Press.

7. Do you know love when you see it?

INSIGHTS: But wait, what is love anyway? Is love even true at all? Or is it the one real truth in existence? How can we know this, and most importantly, is this even knowable at all? Many people who have experienced what we call 'love' believe not only do they know it, but also that they can spot it a mile away. But is this true?

Aloni, M., & Bernieri, F. J. (2004). Is love blind? The effects of experience and infatuation on the perception of love. Journal of Nonverbal Behavior, 28(4), 287-296.

8. Other than adverse events, how does one gain humility?

INSIGHTS: Is it possible to be humble by birth? Or is it the case that some people are just more egotistical than others by birth? Do we only learn to be humble through life experiences, or does it come more naturally to certain people? Can we be humble without learning the hard way, or does it take learning the hard way to instill humility?

Tangney, J. P. (2002). Humility. Handbook of positive psychology, 411-419.

9. What behavior would make you break up with someone on the spot?

INSIGHTS: Is it just plain old rudeness? A constant lack of respect? What would set you off all the way so as to never want to turn back? Is it something that just happened? Or would it be something that was long in the making and then finally, one day, it was the straw that finally broke the camel's back?

Tashiro, T. Y., & Frazier, P. (2003). "I'll never be in a relationship like that again": Personal growth following romantic relationship breakups. Personal Relationships, 10(1), 113-128.

10. Do you truly believe that people can change within their lifetime?

INSIGHTS: Do people change? Can people change? Do people eventually change at some point? And what is considered change? Is change merely the exchange of simple habits, like changing from chewing gum to vaping? Or is change more like a total revamp of one's personality? Can people become totally different people from the person they once were, or is this just a false observation?

Roberts, B. W., Luo, J., Briley, D. A., Chow, P. I., Su, R., & Hill, P. L. (2017). A systematic review of personality trait change through intervention. Psychological Bulletin, 143(2), 117.

11. If, time after time, people keep falling for the same tricks, what, in your opinion, does that say about H. sapiens?

INSIGHTS: This question also could be "Why don't people learn from the past?" or "Why don't people learn from history?" Species-typical behaviors are behaviors that are generally observed with a given species. For example, birds make nests and have distinctive songs. Humans can talk, but monkeys cannot due to the differences with specific connections in the brain. Thus, is it that humans don't want to learn better, or is it that they are not able to?

Haraway, M. M., & Maples, E. G. (1998). Species-typical behavior. *Comparative psychology: A handbook*, 191-197.

Price, M. (2016). Why monkeys can't talk— and what they would sound like if they could. Science Magazine online, Dec, 9.

12. Are you suspicious of those who push to seek advancement in jobs?

INSIGHTS: Are you suspicious, or might you be jealous? Either way, some people advance in the workplace simply because they are determined, responsible, and hard-working. However, others may not be any of these but still may strangely get that promotion that you tried so very hard to get by putting in all those extra hours. What are the true motives of management, in that case, the best interests of the company, of the best interests of themselves?

Buunk, A. P., Zurriaga, R., González-Navarro, P., & Monzani, L. (2016). Attractive rivals may undermine the expectation of career advancement and enhance jealousy. An experimental study. European Journal of Work and Organizational Psychology, 25(6), 790-803.

13. Do you consider yourself to be confident?

INSIGHTS: Would you say you are confident? Or do you think you might be under? Or are you over? Whatever way you might see yourself, what is confidence anyway? Is it just something we delude ourselves with? Or is it something altogether separate in the human psyche?

Bénabou, R., & Tirole, J. (2002). Self-confidence and personal motivation. The quarterly journal of economics, 117(3), 871-915.

14. Why are we pushed, perhaps way too much for our own good, in childhood, to make and have friends?

INSIGHTS: Why is it that we are directed to make friends at a young age? Of course, parents and most people will say that it is because the world requires good relationships, or the ability to form good relationships, in order to be successful. But what if a kid is truly much happier on their own? What if this is not a pathology, but just the way someone is?

Corsaro, W. A. (2003). We're friends, right? Inside kids' culture. Joseph Henry Press.

15. What can't be disputed?

INSIGHTS: In science, because it works in theories, things are constantly held in a state of potential revision. Although scientific laws have been observed to hold over time, there is always the chance that perhaps, the standing theories may need revision. Thus, science always remains disputable, provided there is compelling evidence. So, science aside, is there anything else in the human experience that is above questioning?

Schellenberg, J. L. (2011). The wisdom to doubt. Cornell University Press.

16. What, in theory, can't be tested?

INSIGHTS: Following Karl Popper's Falsification principle, "For a theory to be considered scientific, it must be able to be tested and conceivably proven false." Thus, anything lying outside this realm would likely be something that may not be testable. So, what are those things, exactly?

Popper, K. R. (1963). Science as falsification. Conjectures and refutations, 1(1963), 33-39.

17. If you never had to work again, would you?

INSIGHTS: Was there ever a time where humans didn't work? Or has working been a part of our existence all the way along? Either way, we know that food definitely doesn't come self-prepared, and our hamburgers definitely don't come from the source ready to eat. But those basic things aside, what are you really working for when you go to that job you hate with those toxic co-workers? Surely you're not there for the company.

Statt, D. A. (1994). Psychology and the World of Work. NYU Press.

18. If you could go back to school for anything right now, what would it be?

INSIGHTS: Should you go for what is likely to get you a job? But what if you don't like anything? And what if you don't have a clue about what it is that you like? If you haven't asked yourself these questions before, perhaps you should take some time to ask yourself about what it really is that brings out all the best in you.

Robinson, K. (2009). The element: How finding your passion changes everything. Penguin.

19. What is the difference between religion and philosophy?

INSIGHTS: Is there a difference between religion and philosophy? It can be shown that there are obvious differences between the two. However, what exactly are these? One thing is that religion has personalities and symbolic rituals, whereas philosophy breaks things down to their essence and analyzes them. Still, there might be a degree of overlap. But is there any overlap, really?

Cornford, F. M. (2018). From religion to philosophy. Princeton University Press.

20. Why are some people convinced that what they "feel" is right and that logic doesn't matter?

INSIGHTS: The real question is whether those people truly know if they are right or not. And if they do know that they are not right, then why would they need to act like they are right? Why would someone essentially lie so that they don't have to face admitting they could be wrong?

Von Hippel, W., & Trivers, R. (2011). The evolution and psychology of self-deception. Behavioral and brain sciences, 34(1), 1.

21. Can you name a negative consequence of escapism?

INSIGHTS: The Merriam-Webster Dictionary defines addiction as "a compulsive, chronic, physiological or psychological need for a habit-forming substance, behavior, or activity having harmful physical, psychological, or social effects and typically causing well-defined symptoms (such as anxiety, irritability, tremors, or nausea) upon withdrawal or abstinence: the state of being addicted." Given that this is the definition of addiction, would this be the only possible negative for escapism?

https://www.merriam-webster.com/dictionary/addiction

22. Are you suspicious of people that seem to like to only point out your faults or shortcomings?

INSIGHTS: Some people just hate criticism, period. Others will hear it only from certain people but will write anyone else off. But do any of us like people that have a need to point out only our flaws and nothing else? Is this just us with a filtering bias, or do these people really just concentrate on our shortcomings?

Maisel, E. (2006). Toxic Criticism: Break the Cycle with Friends, Family, Coworkers, and Yourself. McGraw Hill Professional.

23. Are video games healthy?

INSIGHTS: One of the biggest pastimes there is, video games are one of the most popular leisure activities in modern times. And they are also a serious pastime at that. With all sorts of setups and ways to play, whether it be in teams online or even competitions, video games have a significant number of fans. Despite this, however, with anything that can be fun, there is also the potential for adverse behaviors and effects. Thus, are video games really good for us?

Deleuze, J., Long, J., Liu, T. Q., Maurage, P., & Billieux, J. (2018). Passion or addiction? Correlates of healthy versus problematic use of videogames in a sample of French-speaking regular players. Addictive Behaviors, 82, 114-121.

24. Why are there no holidays where we go out and visit science museums and such things?

INSIGHTS: Why are there no holidays dedicated to scientists? Have scientists not had an impact on people and the world? Has not science and innovation done beneficial things for people? If so, then why no holiday?

Coyne, J. A. (2012). Science, religion, and society: the problem of evolution in America. Evolution: International Journal of Organic Evolution, 66(8), 2654-2663.

25. Do you think in the future, using genetic biotechnology, that they will attempt to create real life werewolves and vampires?

INSIGHTS: Right now, we can make fluorescent bacteria and other things. We can also make recombinant insulin and large-scale vaccine synthesis. We can do some pretty cool stuff, but could we ever get to the point where we will make fictional nightmares? Could it ever be possible that we could get to this point? Or is this just all wishful thinking?

Sager, B. (2001). Scenarios on the future of biotechnology. Technological Forecasting and Social Change, 68(2), 109-129.

26. Can you fix 'stupid?'

INSIGHTS: What is stupid exactly, anyway? We all know how to place the word in everyday scenarios, but when we examine the concept with a little depth, a simple definition is not easily found. We all know when to say someone is stupid and to point out when someone is acting stupid, but what exactly IS stupid? And more so, can it be fixed?

Ronell, A. (2002). Stupidity. University of Illinois Press.

27. What are the downsides to a world that has no "common sense?"

INSIGHTS: The Merriam-Webster Dictionary defines it as "Sound and prudent judgment based on a simple perception of the situation or facts." The Cambridge Dictionary defines it as "The basic level of practical knowledge and judgment that we all need to help us live in a reasonable and safe way:" The Collins Dictionary defines it as "Your common sense is your natural ability to make good judgments and to behave in a practical and sensible way." Thus, in a world devoid of common sense, going by the above definitions, what would that world be like?

https://www.merriam-
webster.com/dictionary/common%20sense

https://dictionary.cambridge.org/us/dictiona
ry/english/common-sense

https://www.collinsdictionary.com/us/dictio
nary/english/common-sense

*28. Why do people legitimize those who deny
facts/truth?*

INSIGHTS: You can have an outright liar, a
liar that is unmistakably a liar, and in the right
case, people will go right along with it. Further,
you can have such a liar even elevated to be
seen with legitimacy.   As this is a strange
behavior of people, what exactly is behind all of
this? Do people like all liars? Or do people just
like some liars?

**Grossman, Z., & Van Der Weele, J. J. (2017).
Self-image and willful ignorance in social
decisions. Journal of the European
Economic Association, 15(1), 173-217.**

29. Can you personally prove that there is no objective reality?

INSIGHTS: Objective reality is that which exists independently of the mind.   However, some quantum theorists maintain that there is no such thing and that everything is subjective and depends on the observer.   Therefore, a proof may exist, but is there any way you personally can come up with an instance that refutes the existence of objective reality?

Proietti, M., Pickston, A., Graffitti, F., Barrow, P., Kundys, D., Branciard, C., ... & Fedrizzi, A. (2019). Experimental test of local observer independence. Science advances, 5(9), eaaw9832.

30. Are all ideas original, or is there always some degree of overlap with pre-established ideas?

INSIGHTS: Has someone else thought of my ideas before?   Are all my thoughts and ideas original, or have other people's minds entertained the thoughts I've had before? Have people long ago in the past had ideas that are equivalent to mine? And most importantly, did my ideas come from other people's ideas?

Turner, M. (2014). The origin of ideas: Blending, creativity, and the human spark. Oxford University Press.

31. Are humans able to conceive of all possible concepts?

INSIGHTS: Perhaps, but perhaps not. Moving back down to more practical matters, it is thought that even fields such as medicine are now too complex for the capacity of the human mind. And the things that are known in medicine may be mostly, if not totally comprehendible, but is a single human mind able to "know it all?" Thus, when we move on from human mind capacity to the human mind's limits of conceptualization, is it here that we are strongest? Or are we even less capable in this regard?

Obermeyer, Z., & Lee, T. H. (2017). Lost in thought: the limits of the human mind and the future of medicine. The New England journal of medicine, 377(13), 1209.

32. Is "smart" an illusion?

INSIGHTS: We use the word often, and it's so common that perhaps we take what it may truly mean for granted. That being said, so what is 'smart' anyway? Is it a consistent trait, or is it an intermittent trait? Are we all capable of having smart moments? Are we all capable of being smart at all?

Sternberg, R. J., & Kaufman, J. C. (Eds.). (2013). The evolution of intelligence. Psychology Press.

33. Does true, 100% security exist?

INSIGHTS: Some people live their entire lives playing it safe. They are convinced that to take a risk is to accept danger. However, in this estimate, they often forget that almost everything comes with some sort of risk, at least in theory. Or is it the case that everything does come with risk?

Edlin, G. J. (1986). No Such Thing as No Risk. Bio/Technology, 4(6), 592-592.

34. Does a person get smarter in proportion to the number of books they read, courses they take, plus experiences they engage in?

INSIGHTS: Can anyone simply get smarter by living a bit, reading books, and taking courses? Is it the perfect formula to get smart? And will it work for everyone? Or are there other factors at work when it comes to 'smarts?'

Gray, E., & Tall, D. (2007). Abstraction as a natural process of mental compression. Mathematics Education Research Journal, 19(2), 23-40.

35. Overall, what do you think humans are destined for?

INSIGHTS: Given the collective apathy over critical world issues, many people are of the opinion that the human race doesn't have much of a future ahead of it. However, despite this view, optimists have thought a good deal about the possibilities that could happen in the not-so-distant future. For many, the advancement of Artificial Intelligence technology has big expectations. But is this the only route?

Fukuyama, F. (2004). Transhumanism. Foreign Policy, (144), 42-43.

36. Have you ever examined why you think the way you do?

INSIGHTS: Why do you think the way you do, and why do others think the way they do? Why is it that similar members of a society can have such different views on life, yet, they are from the same society? Is it something internal? Or is it something external? Or is it how we are raised? Or is it something else entirely? Whatever it may be, why do we all think the way we do?

Şimşek, Ö. F., & Yalınçetin, B. (2010). I feel unique, therefore I am: The development and preliminary validation of the personal sense of uniqueness (PSU) scale. Personality and Individual Differences, 49(6), 576-581.

37. Innate notions aside, where do most of your personal ideas come from?

INSIGHTS: In his 2001 article in *Current Opinion in Neurobiology,* Douglas Hofstadter stated that "every concept we have is essentially nothing but a tightly packaged bundle of analogies." Thus, we distill the essence from our ideas, leaving us with an abstract framework, and then use this framework to build with or connect to other ideas. The only question, however, is, "Where do we get our basic analogies that we start this process from?"

Hofstadter, D. R. (2001). Analogy as the core of cognition. *The analogical mind: Perspectives from cognitive science*, **499-538.**

38. Are systems and rankings of people just collective illusions within our intersubjective consciousness?

INSIGHTS: So they got a gold medal. So that other guy got first place. So that lady won the city entrepreneurial award. But, take away the human aspect and what is really there? Is there anything *there*?

Sahlins, M. D. (2008). The Western illusion of human nature. Chicago: Prickly Paradigm Press.

39. Is there a cure for jealousy?

INSIGHTS: If there was ever a more obnoxious human attribute, it still can't hold a candle to jealousy. And jealousy doesn't seem to help things. It seems to only lead to calamity or tragedy. So, could there be a cure for this toxic behavior?

Goldman, E. (1998). Jealousy: Causes and a possible cure. na.

40. Why do people tie so much of others people's value to employment?

INSIGHTS: It seems that people think people are their job. And to some people, that is all other people can be. But is this even close to true? And if it is supposedly true, then exactly how is this figured out to be true?

Kosine, N. R., Steger, M. F., & Duncan, S. (2008). Purpose-centered career development: A strengths-based approach to finding meaning and purpose in careers. Professional School Counseling, 12(2), 2156759X0801200209.

41. Why are "bad guys" so revered?

INSIGHTS: Do people really cheer for the bad guy? Do we really want the villain to be the real winner? Or is this all just more hype that got thrown around at some point?

Lynch, G. (2020). Netflix and Kill: A look at the cultural fascination with infamous killers.

42. Why are certain people popular, and others are not?

INSIGHTS: Why is it that some people gain instant admiration and others do not? Why can't life just make it so that we are all equally admired? One thing that is true is that there always seems to be those people who are instant hits with everyone. Meanwhile, there are always others who are not. But the question is, "Why is it this way?"

Cillessen, A. H., & Rose, A. J. (2005). Understanding popularity in the peer system. Current Directions in Psychological Science, 14(2), 102-105.

43. Why is it that you try to help some people, and they take your kindness as either idiocy or weakness?

INSIGHTS: Some people are strange indeed. You go out of your way for them, only to have them see you as an easy opportunity. Now, why would someone do that, exactly? Is this a good strategy for the future, or just a quick fix with an uncertain future?

Logar, T. (2010). Exploitation as wrongful use: Beyond taking advantage of vulnerabilities. Acta Analytica, 25(3), 329-346.

44. Why do so many people only think something is an issue if it's in the news?

INSIGHTS: Many of the world's issues are ongoing whether or not they get news coverage. It might even be possible that whatever the news channels rank as important that people will take as important. And whatever the news channels don't talk about might be seen as a minor or even non-issue. So why does this happen? What is it that is at work in the human psyche that might be behind this behavior?

Mindich, D. T. (2005). Tuned out: Why

Americans under 40 don't follow the news. Oxford University Press.

45. Do you think that there are people who don't fall for any deception?

INSIGHTS: Are there cues that some people know that give away liars? Or is it that liars might just have obvious shortcomings? Either way, there does seem to be at least one person in the crowd who isn't fooled. However, for that one person, more than often, there are tons more who are fooled. Or are those skeptics just nonconformists who go against the grain with everything?

DePaulo, B. M., Lindsay, J. J., Malone, B. E., Muhlenbruck, L., Charlton, K., & Cooper, H. (2003). Cues to deception. Psychological bulletin, 129(1), 74.

46. What is the difference between a legit theory and a conspiracy theory?

INSIGHTS: The Merriam-Webster Dictionary defines a conspiracy theory as "a theory that explains an event or set of circumstances as the result of a secret plot by usually powerful conspirators." Whereas, for a theory, it defines it as "a plausible or scientifically acceptable general principle or body of principles offered to explain phenomena."

https://www.merriam-webster.com/dictionary/theory

https://www.merriam-webster.com/dictionary/conspiracy%20theory

47. Do humans have their own existence figured out?

INSIGHTS: Some, like the religious, claim that all one needs to know about life is contained in holy texts. Skeptics claim that this is not at all the case and that humans currently do not understand why they do exist. Others also claim that scientific inquiry has led us to some possible answers that may, in fact, be the real reasons for our existence. However, all the groups mentioned here and perhaps others not mentioned are far from agreement as to what is really going on. Or is it that we are confusing things and actually have the answers right in front of us?

Eagleton, T. (2007). The meaning of life.

Oxford University Press.

48. What could be wrong with a start date for the universe/existence/world being 4004 BC?

INSIGHTS: What could be wrong with this? Well, for one, geological data seems to be greatly in opposition to this. It would almost seem that if we took the evidence from geology, we would see that most of the current existence of the world happened all before 4004 BC. So why, then, would someone have used this as the starting date?

Lemaître, G. (1931). The beginning of the world from the point of view of quantum theory. Nature, 127(3210), 706-706.

49. How long do you think it will be till wheel-less hover cars are the norm?

INSIGHTS: By the year 2000, many people were under the impression that flying cars would be the norm. However, such ambitions are largely more complex than is commonly assumed. As engineers work away on the 'how to,' there are also many other considerations that accompany such technology. And with vehicles suspended in air, more safety issues then become necessary to examine. Till then, there are always Maglev trains.

Zhao, C. F., & Zhai, W. M. (2002). Maglev vehicle/guideway vertical random response and ride quality. Vehicle system dynamics, 38(3), 185-210.

50. What are the symptoms of being surrounded by toxic people?

INSIGHTS: It certainly won't be one symptom alone when you're under the influence of the toxic ones. Indeed, these sorts of people may act to sabotage all aspects of your person, from complaining about the brand of ketchup you use to nagging at you in an awkward setting in a public place. But to truly understand the difference, would you know all the things to expect from these people?

MacKenzie, J. (2015). Psychopath free (expanded edition): Recovering from emotionally abusive relationships with narcissists, sociopaths, and other toxic people. Penguin.

51. What is your personal policy about dealing with/interacting with edgy, need-to-walk-on-egg-shells-when-around sort of folk?

INSIGHTS: Some people might be over-sensitive to the point where they can be edgy and irritable. Of course, for the innocent bystander or messenger, this can be a formidable challenge to deal with, given that some of these folks are waiting to go off. Thus, with things being this way, what is your personal view on how to deal with people like this?

Craig, K. J., Hietanen, H., Markova, I. S., & Berrios, G. E. (2008). The Irritability Questionnaire: a new scale for the measurement of irritability. Psychiatry research, 159(3), 367-375.

52. What should science know more about?

INSIGHTS: Is science good where it is covering the things that it covers? Or could it do more? Are there any topics that we are missing that could use to be examined? If so, what are they?

Norman, R. L., Dunning-Davies, J., Heredia-Rojas, J. A., & Foletti, A. (2016). Quantum information medicine: Bit as it—The future

direction of medical science: Antimicrobial and other potential nontoxic treatments. World Journal of Neuroscience, 6(3), 193-207.

53. *Do you question rules?*

INSIGHTS: Do you take everything you are told to be true? Do you think that if something is the way it is, that that IS the way it is? Is everything the way it is because it is the best way it can be or is it that way because no one has really questioned it? Do you think all rules are the best possible ones made for a given situation?

Hernandez, H. Essay: Beliefs in Science.

54. *Why are people convinced that they absolutely must have beliefs?*

INSIGHTS: Do you really have to believe anything? If so, why? Why can't someone just not make up their mind? Why does anyone have to make their mind up? And who said so, and what authority are they?

Dennett, D. (1995). Do animals have beliefs?

Comparative approaches to cognitive science, 111.

55. If squirrels and other animals wrote and read books, do you think so many would end up as roadkill?

INSIGHTS: And just how long do we have to wait before squirrels pick up the necessary cerebral components to conceive of the concept of reading? Will it be in a few years? Or will it be in thousands of years? Or millions of years? And will squirrels last long enough in the future that they will pick up the trait of reading? Or will they never achieve it?

Kumar, S., & Hedges, S. B. (1998). A molecular timescale for vertebrate evolution. Nature, 392(6679), 917-920.

56. Will your legacy have an impact on future generations?

INSIGHTS: We might have the idea that all our efforts and passions may summate in such a way that they will be profound enough to inspire the next generations. However, are we able to predict what will be influential in the times that come after us? More so, will people

Sligte, D. J., Nijstad, B. A., & De Dreu, C. K. (2013). Leaving a legacy neutralizes negative effects of death anxiety on creativity. Personality and Social Psychology Bulletin, 39(9), 1152-1163.

57. What might it imply when it is said that humans never learn from history?

INSIGHTS: It's not hard to notice that many trends and situations are not so much completely *de novo* but rather are simply another round of previously played trends and situations. Although humans are quick to claim that all situations are new and unique, a short dive into the historical literature will demonstrate that many similar situations have happened before. And more so, that people's responses to them were just the same.

Hart, B. L. (2015). Why don't we learn from history? Lulu Press, Inc.

58. What are some falsehoods that the human brain can perpetuate?

INSIGHTS: The brain is known to be fallible. The mere fact that psychologists and psychiatrists exist is a testament to the fact that the brain is far from a perfect organ. The brain is even susceptible to things like substance addiction, bad habits, and even bias. Thus, how are we so sure that the brain is always operating at its very best?

Buonomano, D. (2011). Brain bugs: how the brain's flaws shape our lives. WW Norton & Company.

59. Is it a common trait for humans to enjoy thinking?

INSIGHTS: Does everyone love to just sit in a comfortable chair and to think on and on for hours on end? Or do people find that boring? Or, worse than boring, do some people find thinking a bothersome or even a troublesome experience? Where would you say that people generally stand on thinking?

Dahl, D. W., & Moreau, C. P. (2007). Thinking inside the box: Why consumers enjoy constrained creative experiences. Journal of

Marketing Research, 44(3), 357-369.

60. Where do most people get their notions and concepts from?

INSIGHTS: Are we born with all our ideas? Perhaps we are born with some. But a bit of life experience tends to suggest that we get a good deal of our ideas from external experiences. Then comes the question of how different everyone else is from one another. Am I that different that all my ideas and theories about life are completely opposite and in no way the same to the people around me?

Vandenbosch, B., Fay, S., & Saatçioglu, A. (2001). Where ideas come from: A systematic view of inquiry.

61. Are people "their actions?"

INSIGHTS: Are people what they proclaim? Or are they what they do? Is someone what they dream they are? Or is someone the collection of all the things they've done?

Duffy, J., & Feltovich, N. (2002). Do actions speak louder than words? An experimental

comparison of observation and cheap talk. Games and Economic Behavior, 39(1), 1-27.

62. If alien life was found to be heading to earth within the next month, what would you do?

INSIGHTS: Would you be scared? Would you be happy? Would you get ready with a bouquet and a box of chocolates to greet the incoming beings? Would you hide? Would you run off to a remote area and hope that the whole interaction would blow over quickly? Do you think it would be like in the movies? And most importantly, do you think that these beings might be hostile?

Schulze-Makuch, D., & Irwin, L. N. (2006). The prospect of alien life in exotic forms on other worlds. Naturwissenschaften, 93(4), 155-172.

63. Do you consider yourself someone who has no problem questioning authority?

INSIGHTS: In the face of authority, do you back away and just let things be, or do you bring out your question list? Do you find yourself intimidated, or do you think authority is just illusion and enforcement? Either way, do you question the moves and motives of what the people above you are doing?

Judd, D. M. (2017). Questioning authority: Political resistance and the ethic of natural science. Routledge.

64. Can you go through life without judging anyone?

INSIGHTS: Is it a reflex that we tend to judge things and people? Or is this a learned thing? Either way, could anyone go without judging? Would this be a good idea? Or could there be issues if one does not judge?

Genschow, O., Rigoni, D., & Brass, M. (2017). Belief in free will affects causal attributions when judging others' behavior. Proceedings of the National Academy of Sciences, 114(38), 10071-10076.

65. Will humankind be done with the supernatural within the next 100 years?

INSIGHTS: Will ghosts and vampires ever fade off out of popularity? Will they ever become boring and obsolete to audiences of the future? Will souls and spirits be a thing of the past that people will simply smile at when it is brought up that 'previous peoples' used to believe in such things?

Boudry, M., & Coyne, J. (2016). Disbelief in belief: On the cognitive status of supernatural beliefs. Philosophical Psychology, 29(4), 601-615.

66. Why do people come up with conspiracy theories?

INSIGHTS: Is it entertainment? Or is it a reaction to uncertainty? What is the need to come up with stories that may not even have a shred of truth behind them? Either way, are we that bored that we have a drive to push absurdities over the top? Or are we trying to make sense the best we can with what we have at hand?

Koerth-Baker, M. (2013). Why rational people buy into conspiracy theories. The New York Times Magazine, 21.

67. Do you believe in 'luck?'

INSIGHTS: Some people say they believe in luck; others do not. But if it is not luck, then what is it exactly? What collapses probability into certain events over others? Whatever you wish to call it, luck seems hard to write off as a major factor. Still, however, is there something to the chaos of life we don't know about? Perhaps there is more to luck than luck?'

Rescher, N. (2001). Luck: The brilliant randomness of everyday life. University of Pittsburgh Pre.

68. Did you take more or less risks after you were married with kids?

INSIGHTS: In a study about whether single versus married CEOs took more risks, it was found that single CEOs took more risks than those who were married. However, what impact children have on this is a matter of further inquiry, and also, what about those who are not CEOs?

Roussanov, N., & Savor, P. (2014). Marriage and managers' attitudes to risk. Management Science, 60(10), 2496-2508.

69. What do you hate being questioned?

INSIGHTS: Is it just that questions can be annoying? Or is it because people might disguise their jabs via intentionally crafted questions? But what is it you dislike being questioned? Is it perhaps your more obvious features that people seem to need to point out to the whole world? Or is it your beliefs and ideals? Whatever it may be, what sets you off?

Hornsey, M. J. (2005). Why being right is not enough: Predicting defensiveness in the face of group criticism. European review of social psychology, 16(1), 301-334.

70. Do you think biology explains all of human behavior?

INSIGHTS: Is it all just biology? Like, is that all there is to humans is just biology? Surely most people will want to disagree. But what evidence do we have that it isn't?

Thorpe, W. H. (2018). Animal nature and human nature. Routledge.

71. Do impossibilities truly exist?

INSIGHTS: "Nothing is impossible, Styles!" Sure, that is what people say in theoretical discussions, but is that exactly true?

Stalnaker, R. (1996). Impossibilities. Philosophical Topics, 24(1), 193-204.

72. In the case of people that don't get along, is it that they can't get along or won't get along?

INSIGHTS: Are people making an active point to just not get along for the sake of not getting along? Or are there deeper reasons as to why people don't get along? And what are those reasons? Are they just petty things, or are they significant and important?

Abramowitz, A., & Saunders, K. (2005, June). Why can't we all just get along? The reality of a polarized America. In The Forum (Vol. 3, No. 2, pp. 1-22). bepress.

73. Do you think it's possible that if we work together and stick together, that we could build heaven right here on earth?

INSIGHTS: We fight a lot. And in fact, we might even fight more than we do spend time getting along. But what if we stopped our collective foolery and worked together, appreciating one another? Could we build heaven for everyone right here on earth?

Levitas, R. (2010). The concept of utopia (Vol. 3). Peter Lang.

74. If I am designed to sin, why would I be punished and have to repent?

INSIGHTS: Although there are religious takes on this question, one must wonder at the apparent contradiction of the question above? Or is it that we just don't understand the doctrines and or axioms of those who came up with these ideas? Either way, what is in forgiveness that we seek? For believers, is it damnation? And for non-believers, is it a clear conscience?

Enright, R. D. (1991). The moral development of forgiveness. Handbook of moral behavior and development, 1, 123-152.

75. What has you convinced there is an afterlife?

INSIGHTS: Some people believe in life after death. But since no one has ever come back from death to give a personal testimony, we are sort of left to take a guess at what lies in the great beyond. Of course, there's religion's take on it – that we go to heaven – but still, again, for some people, this still isn't convincing enough.

Bering, J. M. (2006). The cognitive psychology of belief in the supernatural: Belief in a deity or an afterlife could be an evolutionarily advantageous by-product of people's ability to reason about the minds of others. American scientist, 94(2), 142-149.

76. Do you think, given our current state, that we could slip into a second round of dark ages?

INSIGHTS: The fall of the Western Roman Empire is said to be the beginning of the Dark Ages. Thus, are there any other contemporary empires or empire-like structures that have a significant impact on the world? Well, of course, there is! However, given that people are connected differently from 476 AD, it does make one wonder if the same sort of shift could occur in the not-so-distant future?

Gibbon, E., & Milman, H. H. (2003). The decline and fall of the Roman Empire (Vol. 3). New York: Modern library.

77. Do you believe animals have the sense to foresee major natural disasters or weather phenomena?

INSIGHTS: Is it true that animals can sense disastrous weather and other phenomena long before it happens? Is it true that most animals, except humans, can do this? Why do humans need instruments to do something similar?

Woith, H., Petersen, G. M., Hainzl, S., & Dahm, T. (2018). Can animals predict earthquakes? Bulletin of the Seismological Society of America, 108(3A), 1031-1045.

78. Do you backup or confirm your personal knowledge with research?

INSIGHTS: People all have beliefs and personal knowledge. But does anyone ever research their beliefs and knowledge to see if it truly checks out? Of course, there must certainly be people out there who are just fine with their knowledge just the way it is. But, if one was to examine one's own beliefs and knowledge, do you think everything would check out just fine?

Koriat, A. (2018). When reality is out of focus: Can people tell whether their beliefs and judgments are correct or wrong? Journal of Experimental Psychology: General, 147(5), 613.

79. Do you consider yourself robust to the power of mass influence?

INSIGHTS: Do you do your own thing, or do you watch and see what others do? Do you have your own mind or look to the media to see where the best place to stand is? If you continue to do you all while the world goes on all around you, it might be true that you are impervious to the influence of the rest.

Schmitt-Beck, R. (2015). Bandwagon effect. The international encyclopedia of political communication, 1-5.

80. Do you think plants have sentience?

INSIGHTS: Some people think only humans have sentience and consciousness. However, it is beginning to be thought that animals and perhaps plants as well are not only sentient but are conscious. However, the big issue is "How can one tell?" If a plant is indeed sentient, how would one be able to test this? Or do we have it all wrong and have we been missing the obvious all along?

Ginsburg, S., & Jablonka, E. (2021). Sentience in Plants: A Green Red Herring? Journal of Consciousness Studies, 28(1-2), 17-33.

81. Despite the benefits alleged, is it possible that exercise can also be a negative for health?

INSIGHTS: We are constantly told that exercise a necessity for good health. However, like all things that can be good for us, everything seems to have a limit. Thus, is there a point or a situation where exercise is not so beneficial for us?

Eijsvogels, T. M., & Thompson, P. D. (2015). Exercise is medicine: at any dose? Jama, 314(18), 1915-1916.

82. If everyone has an opinion that is equal to all other opinions, then why do most people only trust/run to very few and very select folk for an opinion when it comes to something critical?

INSIGHTS: Sure, we trust our friend Larry when he says that he knows good water when he sees it. But do we trust Larry when he tells us to drink the spring water near a toxic waste plant? Why or why not?

Soll, J. B., & Larrick, R. P. (2009). Strategies for revising judgment: How (and how well) people use others' opinions. Journal of experimental psychology: Learning, memory, and cognition, 35(3), 780.

83. What do you believe in with full certainty?

INSIGHTS: The Cambridge dictionary states that certainty is "something that cannot be doubted." Belief itself is defined by the Cambridge Dictionary as "the feeling of being certain that something exists or is true." Thus, moving forward from this, is there anything you believe in that cannot be doubted?

https://dictionary.cambridge.org/us/dictionary/english/certainty

https://dictionary.cambridge.org/us/dictionary/english/belief

84. Do you ever look up a word to see when it first appeared according to linguistic scholars?

INSIGHTS: Lots of words exist today, but most of the words we know today didn't even exist at one point. In fact, likely, most of the words we know didn't exist at all and are more likely relatively recent inventions. In fact, the English language is quite new and has likely been modified many times since it began.

Shipley, J. T. (1984). The origins of English words. The Wilson Quarterly (1976-), 8(4), 164-170.

85. Where, anatomically, do things like thoughts, beliefs, emotions and perceptions exactly sit in the brain?

INSIGHTS: Where is emotion located in the brain? Is it in one place in the frontal cortex? The temporal lobe? Or is it the Corpus Callosum? Or even better still, is it all of these or a specific combination? Worse would be that it is all and none of these, but rather being some kind of network that runs through a portion of each of these and other parts of brain anatomy. Or is it none of these?

Kragel, P. A., & LaBar, K. S. (2016). Decoding the nature of emotion in the brain. Trends in cognitive sciences, 20(6), 444-455.

86. What is the difference between the quantum interpretation from Heisenberg and Bohr (Copenhagen Interpretation)... and the quantum interpretation of David Bohm?

INSIGHTS: And what of all the other interpretations?   Besides thinking things are waves   and/or   particles   and   wave/particle duality, what is the Schrodinger Equation really saying? Of course, if I look at the "usual" take on it, Niels Bohr says it means one thing, whereas if I look at other interpretations, what are they saying exactly? And what about David Bohm's take on all of this?

Tegmark, M. (1998). The interpretation of quantum mechanics: Many worlds or many words? Fortschritte der Physik: Progress of Physics, 46(6-8), 855-862.

87. What is one clue that something is a definite scam?

INSIGHTS: Are there any clues? But how can one really tell for sure? But surely, there must be some loose end that can lead us to discover whether something is legit or is an outright scam? Although it may seem easy in theory, detecting scams, in reality, is often difficult. After all, time after time, people still fall victim to scams of all sorts.

Whitty, M. T. (2019). Who can spot an online romance scam? Journal of Financial Crime.

88. What should we not be straightforward about?

INSIGHTS: Is there any time that honesty *doesn't* pay? Is there a time where a lie might help us if not even work in our favor in the long run? Does it help us to tell a friend that the dress they are wearing is atrocious? Or that they just aren't cut out to be the neurosurgeon they always dreamed of being? Does disclosing such information truly help us and them? Or is it best to remain quiet in such instances?

McCabe, D., & Trevino, L. K. (2002). Honesty and honor codes. Academe, 88(1), 37.

89. What is the trickiest part of life to get through?

INSIGHTS: It's hard to say off-hand, but one thing that doesn't help this is any part of life where one experiences 'failure.' Failure, of course, was once just thought to be a misfortune. However, after a certain point in history, failure then became tied to being a character trait. Thus, any part of life that includes a concentration of failure, or worse, multiple failures, might be said to be far from ideal.

Sandage, S. A. (2009). Born Losers. Harvard University Press.

90. Do you think the Machiavellian way is a good approach to dealing with people?

INSIGHTS: Machiavelli wrote a book called 'The Prince.' In that book, he detailed what the best moves were for a Prince to make, given the life they would have and the scenarios they would run into. Of course, the book is popular simply because of this fact, namely, that it instructs one on how to rule people. And although one might assume that there are tactics and strategies for keeping people happy, more than often, Machiavelli directs the reader to do quite the opposite.

Geis, F. L., & Moon, T. H. (1981). Machiavellianism and deception. Journal of personality and social psychology, 41(4), 766.

91. How many people in a democracy, do you think, actually understand/know how a democracy ACTUALLY works?

INSIGHTS: Do all people living in a democracy even understand how a democracy works? Of course, people are all ready to launch all sorts of jabs and jeers at the politicians they dislike, but do they even understand the ideas of democracy?

Graham, M. H., & Svolik, M. W. (2020). Democracy in America? Partisanship, polarization, and the robustness of support for democracy in the United States. American Political Science Review, 114(2), 392-409.

92. Are you someone who can shrug anything off, or are you the complete opposite of this?

INSIGHTS: How much does the external world affect you? Can you filter it out? Or does it easily get to you? Can you take the important bits out from the noise, or do you get caught up with the noise?

Reigal, R. E., Moral-Campillo, L., Mier, R. J. R. D., Morillo-Baro, J. P., Morales-Sánchez, V., Pastrana, J. L., & Hernández-Mendo, A. (2020). Physical fitness level is related to attention and concentration in adolescents. Frontiers in psychology, 11, 110.

93. Is all you have truly yours?

INSIGHTS: "You can't take it with you." This is the reply most often encountered when discussing possessions and death. Despite this, people still strive to own things, whether it be a car or a house, or other material items. More so, there is always the possibility that such items can be lost, stolen, or even confiscated. With that as the case, can one say that they truly own anything? Why?

LeFevre, R. (1980). Philosophy of Ownership, The. Ludwig von Mises Institute.

94. If you literally don't care, is this believing?

INSIGHTS: "Believe" is defined by the Cambridge Dictionary as "to think that something is true, correct, or real." Lexico from Oxford defines "don't care" as "A person who does not care; a careless, unconcerned, or indifferent person. These two definitions appear to be completely non-overlapping. Therefore, does the act of not caring have anything to do with believing at all?

https://dictionary.cambridge.org/us/dictionary/english/believe

https://www.lexico.com/en/definition/don%27t-care

95. *Can you name something that can be perfectly neither proven or disproven by science?*

INSIGHTS: Is there anything that science can't test? Or are there things that may indefinitely remain out of reach of the scientific method?

Fishman, Y. I. (2007). Can science test supernatural worldviews? In Science, Worldviews and Education (pp. 165-189). Springer, Dordrecht.

96. Have you ever met someone who did a lot of stuff in life, but didn't seem to take much, if anything, from all of it?

INSIGHTS: On a very slightly different topic, but still quite related, we have the conditions of 'Aphantasia" and "Severely deficient autobiographical memory (SDAM)." These folks don't have any ability for mental imagery, in the case of Aphantasia, and recollection in the case of SDAM. Thus, these are people who really do 'live in the present."

Watkins, N. W. (2018). (A) phantasia and severely deficient autobiographical memory: Scientific and personal perspectives. Cortex, 105, 41-52.

97. Do you think there are people who think that freedom means "I can be as nasty to others as I want to be?"

INSIGHTS: Does freedom mean one can be nasty as they want to be? Is that really what a free and civil society is about? Or do we owe our fellow humans a degree of respect simply because our society is civil and they are our fellow humans?

De Kadt, E. (2005). Abusing Cultural

Freedom: coercion in the name of God. Journal of Human Development, 6(1), 55-76.

98. What is the worst emotion to experience?

INSIGHTS: Surely we're not going to say happiness.   But sadness is definitely a candidate, and so is misery.   But could there be something else that is even worse?

Hayward, C., Killen, J. D., Kraemer, H. C., & Taylor, C. B. (2000). Predictors of panic attacks in adolescents. Journal of the American Academy of Child & Adolescent Psychiatry, 39(2), 207-214.

99. Do you find you tend to meet or exceed expectations or disappoint the people you know?

INSIGHTS: Are you the root of all heartache? Or are you the prime pleaser? And do you try, or do you just happen to get lucky? Either way, where do you think you rate on this?

Van Dijk, W. W., Zeelenberg, M., & Van der Pligt, J. (2003). Blessed are those who expect nothing: Lowering expectations as a

way of avoiding disappointment. *Journal of Economic Psychology, 24(4),* 505-516.

100. Would you consider yourself a leader or a follower?

INSIGHTS: We can be one or the other, or some other shade of grey. But where do you see yourself in this? Some people are leaders, but are the majority followers? And how would one know this?

Owens, B. P., Wallace, A. S., & Waldman, D. A. (2015). Leader narcissism and follower outcomes: the counterbalancing effect of leader humility. Journal of Applied Psychology, 100(4), 1203.

101. Do humans like dogs more than they like other humans?

INSIGHTS: Maybe people do like dogs more than other humans. But where does this behavior come from? It seems that our canine companions have been right beside us for quite some time, and perhaps this has something to do with it? But to the extent that people like dogs more than other people? Is this true?

Why?

Schleidt, W. M., & Shalter, M. D. (2003). Co-evolution of humans and canids. Evolution and cognition, 9(1), 57-72.

102. Do you think what people will and won't spend money on could be considered revealing of their true character?

INSIGHTS: Can we get a conclusive read of someone just from a single transaction? More so, is the collection of the things someone is willing to purchase an indication of their person as a whole? Or is it that people are more complicated than that?

Bilsky, W., & Schwartz, S. H. (1994). Values and personality. European journal of personality, 8(3), 163-181.

103. If you had a Wikipedia page about you, how long do you think the article would be?

INSIGHTS: Have you done enough in life to have a Wikipedia page written about you? If so, how long would it be? Would there be any unique highlights? Or would it be short?

Sanchez-Roige, S., Gray, J. C., MacKillop, J., Chen, C. H., & Palmer, A. A. (2018). The genetics of human personality. Genes, Brain and Behavior, 17(3), e12439.

104. Do we really need people to rule us?

INSIGHTS: Do we need people ruling us? Or is it that we need those rulers because of other people? Or is it because of people like ourselves? Or is this because that is just the system people keep going along with?

Hirshleifer, J. (1995). Anarchy and its breakdown. Journal of Political Economy, 103(1), 26-52.

105. Do you think that there are any historical figures that didn't exist?

INSIGHTS: It is highly speculated that a good number of historical figures may have been fictional. On the big list of doubt, Socrates and even Jesus of Nazareth have their existence in question, despite being held up by the faith of so many of the world's people. Although the two figures mentioned here are definitely on the list, do you know any others who also are doubted to have really existed?

Russell, B. (2013). History of western philosophy: Collectors edition. Routledge.

106. Can you, with confidence, tell the difference between an anthropocentric point of view or idea from one that is not?

INSIGHTS: Do you know the difference between an idea based around the human point of view versus one that is more objective? Can you see the difference between a theory that is based around non-anthropocentric ideas versus one that is completely based around anthropocentric ones?

Preston, J. L., & Shin, F. (2020). Anthropocentric biases in teleological thinking: How nature seems designed for humans. Journal of Experimental Psychology: General.

107. Can it be perfectly proven beyond a shred of a doubt that there are absolutely NO FACTS?

INSIGHTS: Some people are convinced that there are no facts and that everything is fluid.

However, we must ask ourselves, "Is this what we really see?" Are there no consistencies whatsoever in our existence? Even if there were, some might then claim that we just haven't observed things long enough to see them change. But is that even true? Either way, we can construct facts like two plus two equals four, so if we can, why can't the universe do the same?

Mulligan, K., & Correia, F. (2007). Facts.

108. Do you think that it is imperative that people should have at least one hobby?

INSIGHTS: Should people have hobbies? Or should people just get a job? Is a hobby even useful? Or is it just a waste of time? Whatever you may think, the point is that people do have hobbies. But is it beneficial?

Dolan, P. (2014). Happiness by design: Finding pleasure and purpose in everyday life. Penguin UK.

109. If it affects you, is it your business?

INSIGHTS: And even if it wasn't your business, would this change whether it affects you or not? The thing is, there is always some sort of unintended or unwanted side effects from a given thing. For example, we have exhaust from cars. We like the drive, but we don't like the pollution. Now, since pollution affects you, can you say that it is your business?

Nieuwland, S., & Van Melik, R. (2020). Regulating Airbnb: how cities deal with perceived negative externalities of short-term rentals. Current Issues in Tourism, 23(7), 811-825.

110. Would you rather face or ignore reality?

INSIGHTS: Even in the face of facts, people can not only ignore reality but even distort it. After all, not always is a given truth accepted or welcome. Of course, we are all ready to accept beneficial truths or realities, but as for those which are not in our favor, reluctance, if not just flat-out denial, is often our immediate reaction.

Steiner, J. (1985). Turning a blind eye: The cover up for Oedipus. International review of psycho-analysis, 12, 161-172.

111. Can you ever be too determined?

INSIGHTS: Can you be so determined that you defeat yourself? Although it seems that the more determined one is, the more power one would have to get through a given scenario. However, is there a point where it can be too much?

Hodge, B., Wright, B., & Bennett, P. (2018). The role of grit in determining engagement and academic outcomes for university students. Research in Higher Education, 59(4), 448-460.

112. Does the universe really care about us?

INSIGHTS: It is thought by a good number of scholars that the universe is completely indifferent to us and our existence. Of course, on the other side of that, you have religion which asserts the opposite. But why is there evil in the world, and why does it never seem to end? How could something care about us when it allows the potential for bad things to happen to us?

Kahane, G. (2021). Is the Universe Indifferent? Should We Care. Philosophy and Phenomenological Research.

113. If someone wrongly but badly humiliates you, do you just let it go?

INSIGHTS: Are you just going to stand there and take it? Indeed, humiliation is one of the most abrasive experiences one can endure. But why are we so averse to it? Can we train ourselves not to respond to it? Or is it something that we will always find antagonistic and enraging?

Klein, D. C. (1991). The humiliation dynamic: An overview. Journal of Primary Prevention, 12(2), 93-121.

114. Why does disease exist?

INSIGHTS: Of all the things we don't need, disease is definitely one of those things. And nothing does a better job of creating more misery that no one needs than disease. Whether it is an external infectious agent or genetics, humans are cornered on all sides. But the question is, why?

Slingenbergh, J., Gilbert, M., Balogh, K. D., & Wint, W. (2004). Ecological sources of zoonotic diseases. Revue scientifique et technique-Office international des épizooties, 23(2), 467-484.

115. Did you ever have any friends that just wanted to be told only what they wanted to hear?

INSIGHTS: Are we friends with our friends because we share common views? Or do you have friends with diverse views? Do you have to agree with people's views before you will befriend them? Or do you reject anyone who does not have the same outlook on things as you do?

Cinelli, M., Morales, G. D. F., Galeazzi, A., Quattrociocchi, W., & Starnini, M. (2021). The echo chamber effect on social media. Proceedings of the National Academy of Sciences, 118(9).

116. Guardian Angels: Do they exist?

INSIGHTS: Many people believe that they are watched over and protected by Guardian Angels. Whether this is fact or fiction does not take away the fact that many people are convinced that such entities exist. But is there truth to the existence of real Guardian Angels? Or is it that this is merely a coping mechanism?

Büssing, A., Reiser, F., Michalsen, A., Zahn, A., & Baumann, K. (2015). Do patients with

chronic pain diseases believe in guardian angels: Even in a secular society? A cross-sectional study among german patients with chronic diseases. Journal of religion and health, 54(1), 76-86.

117. Have you ever had a young/mid/old or any other sort of life crisis?

INSIGHTS: Have you ever come to a point where everything seemed doubtful or disappointing? When did you feel as if you just wanted to go back to better times and toss the current ones? Of course, if you are feeling this, you should likely call SAMHSA's National Helpline: 1-800-662-HELP (4357). However, if you ever recall feeling like this, it might be possible that you have had a crisis of some sort. Take care to acquaint yourself with the signs and symptoms.

Brim Jr, O. G. (1976). Theories of the male mid-life crisis. The Counseling Psychologist, 6(1), 2-9.

118. How far into the future do you envision your plans, goals and dreams?

INSIGHTS: At some point in our lives, we envision a future for ourselves. Depending on the timescale used, this can mean getting off the couch and going to the store for a bag of chips, or it can mean our career goal of becoming CEO of the Biotech company we always wanted to start. Whatever it is we choose to do, to what extent do you have it all mentally planned out?

Atance, C. M., & O'Neill, D. K. (2001). Episodic future thinking. Trends in cognitive sciences, 5(12), 533-539.

119. Do you find that people tend to overcomplicate things?

INSIGHTS: Nicholas Nassim Taleb has an idea he calls "The Noise Bottleneck." This essentially means that the more data one takes in, the amount of signal decreases while the noise in the data you take in increases. Now this theory doesn't necessarily directly address the question, but if you think about it, when we over-describe something or add in more detail, are we adding more signal, or are we just adding more noise? And is it possible to entirely drown out the signal with noise?

Taleb, N. N. (2012). Antifragile: Things that gain from disorder (Vol. 3). Random House Incorporated.

120. Why do you suppose people praise others for their stance rather than their content?

INSIGHTS: What if someone is a great singer that you admire, but they like the political party you hate? Are they still a good singer, then? Or should they be booted out of business? Or what if someone made the cure for a terrible disease but supported the political party that you dislike? Would you have any admiration for them?

Gillani, N., Yuan, A., Saveski, M., Vosoughi, S., & Roy, D. (2018, April). Me, my echo chamber, and I: introspection on social media polarization. In Proceedings of the 2018 World Wide Web Conference (pp. 823-831).

121. Is craving attention or needing praise and/or clout a behavioral thing, an addiction, or a pathology?

INSIGHTS: Do we really need praise? Or did our well-intentioned parents just condition us this way? Or is it innate? Or pathological?

Harter, S. (1993). Causes and consequences of low self-esteem in children and adolescents. In Self-esteem (pp. 87-116). Springer, Boston, MA.

122. What is it about the word 'evidence' that scares so many people?

INSIGHTS: People might say "evidence-schmevidence!" But do they really mean that if they were up against a judge who would let them off the charges against them should they be able to prove that they were innocent via evidence?

Anglin, S. M. (2019). Do beliefs yield to evidence? Examining belief perseverance vs. change in response to congruent empirical findings. Journal of Experimental Social Psychology, 82, 176-199.

123. Do you think that the 'modern' world, although having definite positives, is a bit more than humans are evolved to handle?

INSIGHTS: Have we changed from the first few H. sapiens, or are we the same as we have always been, ever since we were a distinct species? And if so, is a creature with an origin from ~300,000 years ago able to deal with things just fine 300,000 years later? From using stone tools all the way to using laptop computers, is H. sapiens able to handle the environment it has created for itself?

Shea, J. J. (2011). Homo sapiens is as Homo sapiens was: Behavioral variability versus "behavioral modernity" in Paleolithic archaeology. Current anthropology, 52(1), 1-35.

124. The human sense of shame: Have we lost it, or was it always a rare bird?

INSIGHTS: Do people feel shame for things that they may have done erroneously? More so, do people feel shame for things they might have done that affected others negatively, all for the advancement of their own best interests? What conditions internal or external act to remove shame from a person's conscience? More so, has the sense of shame increased or decreased over time, or was it always the same?

Scheff, T. J. (2003). Shame in self and society. Symbolic interaction, 26(2), 239-262.

125. How far back do you know your family history?

INSIGHTS: Censuses have been around at least since ancient times. However, continuous censuses in the United Kingdom have gone on every ten years since 1801, with the exception of 1941. Thus, if one has ancestors from the British Isles, one may only use theoretically be able to use the data from the national archives till 1801. After that, parish records are the only other source, but even these may only extend as far back as the late middle ages. Thus, how might one go back further past this point?

https://www.nationalarchives.gov.uk/help-with-your-research/research-guides/census-records/

126. Do you believe that only things that have been tested by science can be considered as fact?

INSIGHTS: Can facts be guessed or assumed and simply validated because people want it to be that way? Or is that not what validation is? Should we test the things we wish to believe? Or should we just assume things, despite the reputation that the act of assuming comes with?

Godler, Y., & Reich, Z. (2013). How journalists "realize" facts: Epistemology in practice at press conferences. Journalism Practice, 7(6), 674-689.

127. What do you think would happen if inheritance was abolished?

INSIGHTS: Uh-oh! Who would be rich then? Would the wealthy move differently if this was the case? What would people have to start doing in such a world?

Halliday, D. (2018). Inheritance of wealth: Justice, equality, and the right to bequeath. Oxford University Press.

128. What do you consider a power trip?

INSIGHTS: More so, why do people power trip? Some ideas on this are that once in secure positions, people are free from accountability. Thus, anything they do will be free of repercussions and will not come back to haunt them. Thus, who is the most likely person to throw a power trip? Someone who is at the top, or someone who has no authority or power over others? And still, more so, will someone who begins with no power but rises to power end up abusing that power?

Lehrer, J. (2010). The power trip. Power.

129. What things do some people race to cry victim over, but are actually all their own fault?

INSIGHTS: Are all people who don't get their way victims? What is a real victim exactly? Surely, there are many true victims, but where do we draw the line? Or even better yet, can we draw the line? Who are we to judge what someone has had to endure? And is it true that what one might find to be a mere papercut, another might experience as a fatal wound?

Best, J. (1997). Victimization and the victim industry. Society, 34(4), 9-17.

130. What started the trend of accusations becoming convictions?

INSIGHTS: It almost seems that because someone points a finger that it makes someone immediately guilty. Although we all know this isn't true, it certainly doesn't seem to be the case these days.

Dolezal, L., Rose, A., & Cooper, F. (2021). COVID-19, online shaming, and health-care professionals. The Lancet, 398(10299), 482-483.

131. IYI = Idiot Yet Intellectual. What do you consider an IYI?

INSIGHTS: What is the idiot yet intellectual? Are these people that are smart but don't have street smarts? Or are these people who hold high positions but are not at the expected level of intelligence? Either way, this term was invented for a reason, but is the reason legit, or is it just a bad idea?

Taleb, N. N. (2020). Skin in the game: Hidden asymmetries in daily life. Random House Trade Paperbacks.

132. How did entitlement start?

INSIGHTS: This is a hard call, as it may have always been a feature of human behavior. However, in the last twenty or so years, a rise in entitlement has been noted, and along with it, a focus on self-admiration. With the rise of social media, cosmetic surgery, grade inflation, large debts, and inflated self-esteem, although it may be hard to trace the exact origin of entitlement for humanity, it may not be so hard to trace the root of where entitlement became much more prominent. Can you pinpoint exactly where the recent trends originated?

Twenge, J. M., & Campbell, W. K. (2009). Living in the age of entitlement: The narcissism epidemic.

133. Do you think there really is a difference between generations?

INSIGHTS: The Greatest Generation, Baby Boomers, Gen X, Millennials, and Gen Z. Do any of these labels have any sort of justification for their existence? Is there truly any difference between these generations? Do the times and circumstances one grows up with truly shape the individual to an appreciable extent? Is there really a difference between people on the scales of generations?

Glass, A. (2007). Understanding generational differences for competitive success. Industrial and commercial training.

134. Professionals snooping Social Media accounts... Is this professional behavior by professional people?

INSIGHTS: Is it okay for just anyone to snoop your social media accounts? More so, is this a legitimate thing to do? Is it okay for employers to snoop on your social media? Furthermore, should anyone be allowed to snoop your social media in order to get an idea of "who you really are?"

McPeak, A. (2014). Social media snooping and its ethical bounds. Ariz. St. LJ, 46, 845.

135. Do you think a newly confirmed nihilist is someone who has figured it all out, or someone who is but a mere rookie with philosophy?

INSIGHTS: "That's it, there's nothing, there's no point." If this is all someone is concluding with following their first big eureka moment with a book on nihilism, is this someone who has it all figured out? Or is this conclusion naïve? Is there a point to the universe and existence? Or is there none? Either way, is the conclusion that there is no point an enlightened one, or is it not even close to what the real story is?

Gillespie, M. A. (1995). Nihilism before Nietzsche. University of Chicago Press.

136. What do you owe people?

INSIGHTS: Do we owe each other anything? Do we owe each other nothing? Can I just slam a door in someone's face because it is convenient for me to get on with my tasks? Should I just worry only about myself in every single scenario that life presents me with?

Calhoun, C. (2000). The virtue of civility. Philosophy & public affairs, 29(3), 251-275.

137. If someone who lacks empathy is a psychopath, then what is someone who lacks self-reflection?

INSIGHTS: What is it called when someone cannot take a good look at themselves and contemplate their circumstance? Is this a condition? It might very well be part of a known condition, but is it considered a condition all on its own?

Dimaggio, G., Vanheule, S., Lysaker, P. H., Carcione, A., & Nicolò, G. (2009). Impaired self-reflection in psychiatric disorders among adults: a proposal for the existence of a network of semi independent functions. Consciousness and cognition, 18(3), 653-664.

138. Do you think it is somehow possible to avoid 'growing up?'

INSIGHTS: Is it possible, in a world that demands that bills must be paid and that one must have some level of accountability, to not grow up? Is there any way one can deflect the many tests of patience and maturity that adulthood mandates and still be the person they were when they were ten years old? In a world where everyone eventually accepts the conditions of adulthood, like it or not, how can someone resist the mighty current that is left by everyone else and not get swept up into adulthood?

Kiley, D. (1983). The Peter Pan syndrome: Men who have never grown up (p. 298). New York: Dodd, Mead.

139. Are "armchair experts" a source of disinformation?

INSIGHTS: Does that armchair expert bring anything new to the table? Or is it just a pontification session? Is bona fide knowledge being passed on, or is it disinformation?

Jaiswal, J., LoSchiavo, C., & Perlman, D. C. (2020). Disinformation, misinformation and inequality-driven mistrust in the time of COVID-19: lessons unlearned from AIDS denialism. AIDS and Behavior, 24, 2776-2780

140. Would you say that you are just like everyone else?

INSIGHTS: Individualism is defined in Britannica as a "political and social philosophy that emphasizes the moral worth of the individual." Collectivism is defined in Britannica as "any of several types of social organization in which the individual is seen as being subordinate to a social collectivity such as a state, a nation, a race, or a social class." Thus, to truly determine this, it would involve being able to see if you do things that are in common with a group or collective or whether you have your own way of doing things. Of course, by having some things in common with a collective and perhaps some things not, this may not be so straightforward to answer.

https://www.britannica.com/topic/individualism

https://www.britannica.com/topic/collectivism

141. Does ego have any benefits?

INSIGHTS: Is ego just a downward spiral? If so, then why did nature bestow all of us with it? Of course, we've all become acquainted at one point or another with someone who surely could use to have a lot less ego. But what are the advantages of this mental mechanism, given that we all seem to have at least a bit of one?

Vohs, K. D., Baumeister, R. F., Schmeichel, B. J., Twenge, J. M., Nelson, N. M., & Tice, D. M. (2014). Making choices impairs subsequent self-control: a limited-resource account of decision making, self-regulation, and active initiative.

142. Are there more 'bona fide' experts in the world, or more armchair experts in the world?

INSIGHTS: According to the US census, there were 4.5 million people who held Doctoral degrees in 2018. The US population in 2018 was 327.2 million. Thus, a quick shot at the math will give us a rough estimate of the proportions of true experts versus the rest of the population. However, how many of those in the actual population minus the Doctoral degree holders could be considered "arm-chair experts?" The Urban Dictionary defines an armchair expert as "Someone who claims to know all the answers to a problem, situation or scenario but has little or no experience or real understanding of it."

https://www.census.gov/data/tables/2018/demo/education-attainment/cps-detailed-tables.html

https://www.urbandictionary.com/define.php?term=Armchair%20Expert

143. Is social media simply a tool, or something that should come with a warning label?

INSIGHTS: Is social media a harmless thing? If so, then can we say that no one has been harmed by it? Or is there a potential for harm? And what if it wasn't harmful but addictive? Wouldn't this be an issue?

Vogel, E. A., Rose, J. P., Roberts, L. R., & Eckles, K. (2014). Social comparison, social media, and self-esteem. Psychology of popular media culture, 3(4), 206.

144. If in our society 'brainwashing' is a common thing, would you know how you were brainwashed?

INSIGHTS: We assume we are acting on our own thoughts and decisions. But a closer examination of the things we believe will soon reveal much of what we know was learned from someone or something else. Hence, what were those things? And where did those things get the information that they had from? If we think about it, is everything really as it seems? Or have we been led to think this way?

Hunter, E. (1956). What brainwashing is.

145. Are your friends somehow a reflection of you?

INSIGHTS: Is the company I keep somehow a reflection of who I am? Do birds of the same feather really flock together? Or am I able to be around people and not be influenced whatsoever by any of them? Or is there more to the story when it comes to the company I keep?

Curry, O., & Dunbar, R. I. (2013). Do birds of a feather flock together? Human nature, 24(3), 336-347.

146. Why did the universe have to add consciousness to itself?

INSIGHTS: Why do we have consciousness? As we seem to be an embedded part of the universe, we have to ask why it is that we are conscious? What purpose does it serve us to be conscious?

Dehaene, S., Lau, H., & Kouider, S. (2017). What is consciousness, and could machines have it?. Science, 358(6362), 486-492.

147. Do you believe that you have an eye for talent?

INSIGHTS: Although one might be convinced that one does, one has to ask what talent really is in the first place. Is talent the person born with the capability? Or is it the person who has no specific aptitudes but works hard? And then furthermore, what about dedication? Will someone who is dedicated grow and eventually rise above all the rest?

Ulrich, D., & Smallwood, N. (2012). What is talent?. Leader to leader, 2012(63), 55-61.

148. Do you know why colors exist?

INSIGHTS: Color is known to all humans who have the ability to view this phenomenon. While playing around with prisms, Isaac Newton was able to demonstrate that white light is composed of a series of wavelengths of light which we see as distinct colors. However, it is not only light itself but even common objects that can appear to us as having some sort of color. Even though this is a common experience, what makes this happen?

Boccardi, E. (2013). Are Colors Real? Nietzsche: Science and Truth Danny Smith Arqueología: arte, historia, antropología. Análisis filosófico de la génesis y desarrollo de una disciplina, 111.

149. If you had to choose, would you rather be 'tired' or 'bored?'

INSIGHTS: Would you rather be stuck in a fatigued state, or would you rather be just plain old bored? Which one do you find easier to endure? Also, which one do you find you run into most often? Although being chronically tired might indicate something wrong with one's physiology, boredom is more of a strange beast.

Either way, which do you prefer if you had to choose?

Sharpe, M., & Wilks, D. (2002). Fatigue. Bmj, 325(7362), 480-483.

Martin, M., Sadlo, G., & Stew, G. (2006). The phenomenon of boredom. Qualitative Research in Psychology, 3(3), 193-211.

150. What's something you don't believe in that most people believe in?

INSIGHTS: One major thing people believe in is religion. Indeed, an estimate claimed that there were 5.8 billion religious adults, representing 84% of the 2010 world population of 6.9 billion. However, even things like consumerism are thought of by some to be 'religions' in their own sense, thus widening the choices of things people believe in beyond just conventional religion. Thus, is there anything that you believe in that most other people do not?

Hackett, C., Grim, B., Stonawski, M., Skirbekk, V., Potančoková, M., & Abel, G. (2012). The global religious landscape. Washington, DC: Pew Research Center.

Kurenlahti, M., & Salonen, A. O. (2018). Rethinking consumerism from the perspective of religion. Sustainability, 10(7), 2454.

151. Do you think the system that you currently live in is as close to perfect as it can be? Or can you imagine something better?

INSIGHTS: Are we in the perfect ideal configuration for the happiness of all humans? Or are we far from ideal? Are we close for some but far off the mark for others? Is this system the best we can do, or do people just say that because they don't want to think about it?

Vieira, F. (2010). The concept of utopia. The Cambridge companion to utopian literature, 3-27.

152. If you had to guess, do you think that consciousness is more of a set, definite program, or a set of parallel conditions?

INSIGHTS: What parts of the brain are exactly working together to give us consciousness? Is it some of the brain or the whole brain? And what parts are running where? Is it the combined electricity of the brain as it flows from place to place? Or is it the combined electricity constantly being produced and registered by all the different areas of the brain?

Godwin, D., Barry, R. L., & Marois, R. (2015). Breakdown of the brain's functional network modularity with awareness. Proceedings of the National Academy of Sciences, 112(12), 3799-3804.

Cruse, H., & Schilling, M. (2014). Mental states as emergent properties: From walking to consciousness. Open MIND. Frankfurt am Main: MIND Group.

153. Would you rather have been born knowing everything there is to know?

INSIGHTS: Many philosophers have noted that we likely start off as a 'tabula rasa' or 'blank slate.' That is to say, we are born with no knowledge and that our knowledge is gained as we live. If one was to be born in the opposite situation, that is, to be born knowing everything, would this be better? Or maybe the better question would be, "Is that even possible?"

Kalisman, N., Silberberg, G., & Markram, H. (2005). The neocortical microcircuit as a

tabula rasa. Proceedings of the National Academy of Sciences, 102(3), 880-885.

154. Do you think you have good celebrity potential?

INSIGHTS: Could you be a celebrity? If so, why? What do you have to offer? And if you have something to offer people, how long do you think it would last? A lifetime? Or less?

Kurzman, C., Anderson, C., Key, C., Lee, Y. O., Moloney, M., Silver, A., & Van Ryn, M. W. (2007). Celebrity status. Sociological theory, 25(4), 347-367.

155. Are you for, or against, playing it safe in life?

INSIGHTS: A big issue with life is that not all risks are obvious. For example, is getting out of bed in the morning completely devoid of all possible risks? Likely not, as one could easily slip and break a bone or worse. Even just going to the bathroom comes with the risk of being electrocuted should you use a hairdryer or similar appliance. All this, and we haven't even stepped into the kitchen yet. And let's not even talk about getting to work in the morning.

Wilson, R. (1990). Analyzing the daily risks of life. Readings in risk, 57.

156. How would someone know if they were a deep person or a shallow person?

INSIGHTS: Do you really know if someone is a shallow person? If so, how? What are the signs and symptoms? Or, are they not revealing their true selves and just hiding the fact that they might have a serious degree of personal depth?

Kim, J. W., & Chock, T. M. (2017). Personality traits and psychological motivations predicting selfie posting behaviors on social networking sites. Telematics and Informatics, 34(5), 560-571.

157. Why do humans need leisure?

INSIGHTS: It might have been true that before the advent of agriculture, that humans may have spent a great deal of time engaged in leisure activities. With the agricultural revolution, however, more work time might have been required, thus reducing leisure time. So, are we a leisurely creature by nature, who has complicated things by the invention of farming? Or is it just how we view work?

Just, P. (1980). Time and leisure in the elaboration of culture. Journal of Anthropological Research, 36(1), 105-115.

158. Have you ever been written off after doing something well or extraordinary with someone saying, "Yeah, sure, I could do that too if I wanted...?"

INSIGHTS: Jealousy and envy often find themselves manifested in crudely disguised remarks. It is not uncommon to have talents or goals met with sneers or cynical remarks rather than with praise or acclaim. But why do some people opt for negative comments and reactions instead of positive ones?

Van de Ven, N. (2017). Envy and admiration: Emotion and motivation following upward social comparison. Cognition and Emotion, 31(1), 193-200.

159. Why, over time, have our names come to have less and less meaning within them?

INSIGHTS: Is this actually the case, though? Are most of our contemporary names devoid of meaning? Is it just certain cultures who bestow their children names with meanings or is it that we truly don't have any meaning to our names? And if so, why is this the case?

Bramwell, E. S. (2016). Personal names and anthropology. In The Oxford handbook of names and naming.

160. Who is the funniest person you know, whether they are a celebrity or not?

INSIGHTS: What exactly makes someone funny in the first place? And are 'funny people' always funny, or is it just situational or contextual? Either way, comedians exist, and some people prefer one over another, yet some other people like them all, while others don't like any at all.

Zillmann, D. (2000). Humor and comedy. Media entertainment: The psychology of its appeal, 37-57.

161. Given that change is supposedly the only constant in the universe, what in your opinion is the slowest thing in the universe?

INSIGHTS: ^{124}Xe decay is likely the slowest thing known with a half-life value (The time it takes for ½ of a sample of ^{124}Xe to decay) of 1,660,000,000,000,000,000,000 (1.66 x 10^{21}) years.

Mei, D. M., Marshall, I., Wei, W. Z., & Zhang, C. (2014). Measuring double-electron capture with liquid xenon experiments. *Physical Review C, 89*(1), 014608.

162. Would you consider yourself competent at being able to tell if you are getting pulled into something that is neither in your best interest nor is your concern?

INSIGHTS: Are you able to quickly discern whether you are being directed to something beneficial or something that is merely a waste of time? With cellphones, computers, and the internet, it is likely that there has never been a time with more potential for distraction than the current one. Thus, how quickly are you able to brush off things that are not at all in your best interest?

Mark, G., Iqbal, S., & Czerwinski, M. (2017, September). How blocking distractions affects workplace focus and productivity. In Proceedings of the 2017 ACM International Joint Conference on Pervasive and Ubiquitous Computing and Proceedings of the 2017 ACM International Symposium on Wearable Computers (pp. 928-934).

163. Space is expanding... But what is it expanding into?

INSIGHTS: What is the universe expanding into? Well, apparently, it is expanding, but it is thought that it is not expanding into anything. More so, it's thought that it is more like the surface of an expanding balloon. But still, doesn't an inflating balloon expand into *something*? Either way, cosmologists have their theories about what is going on with this expansion of our finite universe.

Ellis, G. F. (2003). The shape of the Universe. Nature, 425(6958), 566-567.

164. Can you name something that is faster than light?

INSIGHTS: We are told that the speed of light is as fast as anything will go in the universe. But is this only because we have never seen anything go faster?

Ehrlich, R. (2003). Faster-than-light speeds, tachyons, and the possibility of tachyonic neutrinos. American Journal of Physics, 71(11), 1109-1114.

165. If we live and experience different realities, then why does gravity pull us all down in the exact same way?

INSIGHTS: Do some of us float and others just stay on the ground? Are people subject to the physical laws differently? And if they claim so, is this just for attention, or is it legit? And if it is legit, how do we know and test that? Or does gravity really have the same effect on all of us?

Fine, K. (2002). The question of realism. In Individuals, Essence and Identity (pp. 3-48). Springer, Dordrecht.

166. Is having a solid grasp of reality in a way, a 'privilege?'

INSIGHTS: Cognitive Impairment is likely more prevalent than is commonly thought. However, what are the exact numbers? And what are those numbers worldwide? Are we all going to make it to the ripe old age of 99 with all of our cognition perfectly intact?

Plassman, B. L., Langa, K. M., Fisher, G. G., Heeringa, S. G., Weir, D. R., Ofstedal, M. B., ... & Wallace, R. B. (2008). Prevalence of cognitive impairment without dementia in the United States. Annals of internal medicine, 148(6), 427-434.

167. Are you able to tell if someone is just telling you what you want to hear as opposed to talking to you straight?

INSIGHTS: People can spice things up to the point of perfect deception. Of course, if you know better, you'll be able to tell what the real message is before their spiel is finished. However, what exactly do you need to know in order to do this?

Hardin, G. (1985). Filters against folly. Viking Books.

168. Have you ever asked yourself why you believe what you believe?

INSIGHTS: How did you come to believe what you believe? Did someone tell you? Did you just make it up? Did you read it somewhere? Or did you go through a series of experiences that you used to construct your personal worldview?

Nilsson, N. J. (2014). Understanding beliefs. MIT Press.

169. We all likely know an "Energy Vampire" or more. But exactly what is it that makes them this way?

INSIGHTS: Those people that drain you and seem to walk off invigorated, all while leaving you desperate for energy, are not creatures of the light. Rather, since they have a peculiar similarity to a popular fictional monster, they have earned themselves the name "Energy Vampires." Indeed, these people will leave an empathic person reaching for energy after even a simple encounter. Despite all this, however, since no bite to the neck transmits this condition, how is it that people come to be such 'creatures?'

Northrup, C. (2018). Dodging Energy Vampires: An Empath's Guide to Evading Relationships that Drain You and Restoring Your Health and Power. Hay House.

170. Do you think a person can avoid facing 'the truths' for an entire lifetime?

INSIGHTS: First thing most people do is question what truth is. Of course, from here, one gets off course pretty fast as now everyone thinks that truth may not exist. But then we think about how we need oxygen and need to breathe. Then a truth suddenly appears.

DeNicola, D. R. (2017). Understanding ignorance: The surprising impact of what we don't know. Mit Press.

171. Do you know what is meant by the saying "Having skin in the game?"

INSIGHTS: Having skin in the game basically means having something to lose. This, of course, refers to situations like having an engineer design a plane and having him fly in its maiden flight. Other things would be like having universities reimburse tuition to any graduates who don't get a job after a given number of years. Another example would be having a politician held accountable for any bad legislature and being forced to pay out of their own pocket for any damages incurred. However, skin in the game goes far beyond these examples. Can you think of any instances where it applies?

Taleb, N. N. (2020). Skin in the game: Hidden asymmetries in daily life. Random House Trade Paperbacks.

172. What would be your advice to someone who is entitled, but doesn't know any better, and finds themselves not getting anywhere in life?

INSIGHTS: What about that person who can't see themselves as their own worst enemy? What is it about their perspective that renders them blind to their own doings? Better still, how would you be able to get across to them that perhaps the external world is not as guilty as they would like to think it is? What would you say to get someone in this predicament to turn around?

Hixon, J. G., & Swann, W. B. (1993). When does introspection bear fruit? Self-reflection, self-insight, and interpersonal

choices. Journal of personality and social psychology, 64(1), 35.

173. What are some things that people hate to admit and will steer away from at any cost?

INSIGHTS: Are there true things that people just don't like to be reminded about? Are there true and factual things you can say to people that they will outright deny and even get mad at you just for bringing it up?

Gilbert, P. (2019). Distinguishing shame, humiliation and guilt: An evolutionary functional analysis and compassion focused interventions. In The bright side of shame (pp. 413-431). Springer, Cham.

174. What is 'light?'

INSIGHTS: "It's a particle!" "It's a wave!" Although we have plenty of mental schematics to follow, what is light, really? As certain experiments demonstrate that it has the behavior of both particles and waves, it goes to ask if light is perhaps even more than this?

Leonhardt, U. (1997). Measuring the

quantum state of light (Vol. 22). Cambridge university press.

175. Do you trust that medications are always prescribed in your best interests?

INSIGHTS: Do doctors always make the right call? Are all your medications exactly what you need and no more and no less? Are doctors giving you the best possible treatment that they know?

Velo, G. P., & Minuz, P. (2009). Medication errors: prescribing faults and prescription errors. British journal of clinical pharmacology, 67(6), 624-628.

176. Now that you've lived a good chunk of life, how much do you believe in good school grades?

INSIGHTS: Most university professors will certainly say that grades are the one true measure of future intelligence and success. But are they, really? Is that to say those who don't get good grades are forever banished to the world of mediocrity and failure?

Jones, D. L. (2011). Academic dishonesty: Are more students cheating? Business Communication Quarterly, 74(2), 141-150.

177. Why do humans "worship?"

INSIGHTS: One theory by Professor Matthew Rossano posits that humans 90,000 – 60,000 years before present began to develop more complex social bonding rituals that eventually came to include the supernatural. As these rituals developed in complexity, those bonded together by such rituals achieved a selection advantage over those groups who did not have such strong group ties.

Rossano, M. (2009). The African Interregnum: The "where,""when," and "why" of the evolution of religion. In *The biological evolution of religious mind and behavior* (pp. 127-141). Springer, Berlin, Heidelberg.

178. What is the best 'state of mind' to go through life with?

INSIGHTS: Is life best lived being grumpy every day? Or is it best lived being the happy-go-lucky Pollyanna? Either way, for those looking to have a fulfilling life, surely not all approaches can work, given that many are antagonistic to one another. So what is the best attitude to face life with? Which one of these ways is the best way for a fulfilling life?

Carver, C. S., Scheier, M. F., & Segerstrom, S. C. (2010). Optimism. Clinical psychology review, 30(7), 879-889.

Dolinski, D., Gromski, W., & Zawisza, E. (1987). Unrealistic pessimism. The Journal of Social Psychology, 127(5), 511-516.

179. Do you think that unemployment will forever be a problem with the human race?

INSIGHTS: Unemployment seems like it's never going away. And politicians go on and on about it as if they are going to fix it, but alas, that never happens. Could it just be that this is the way things are?

Frey, C. B., & Osborne, M. (2013). The future of employment.

180. Do you think the following is a 'word-trick,' or does it symbolize a bona fide trait of reality? "Nothing is still something."

INSIGHTS: Is nothing actually something? As it is a choice in and of itself, although it may represent nothing, it still can be considered to be an option or choice, can it not? Either way, in our day-to-day experience, are things considered nothing actually something? And is that something of any importance? Or is it all just nothing (Which is still something)?

Landis, R. S., James, L. R., Lance, C. E., Pierce, C. A., & Rogelberg, S. G. (2014). When is nothing something? Editorial for the null results special issue of Journal of Business and Psychology. Journal of Business and Psychology, 29(2), 163-167.

181. In your opinion, what is the greatest set-back one can experience in life?

INSIGHTS: The Collins Dictionary defines setback as "An event that delays your progress or reverses some of the progress that you have made." The MacMillan Dictionary defines it as "a problem that delays or that stops progress or makes a situation worse." So, one entry seems to see it as a reversal or a delay, while the other sees it as a delay or a stop. Thus, besides death, what could halt somebody's plans in life to the extent that they would never be able to carry on?

https://www.collinsdictionary.com/us/dictionary/english/setback

https://www.macmillandictionary.com/us/dictionary/american/setback

182. Have you ever been bored with life?

INSIGHTS: Boredom seems to be more of a modern problem due to the fact that we have a lot more time away from work. Indeed, our ancestors likely didn't have much time to be bored as the threat of starvation was real in a world where a successful harvest was a dice toss. Either way, have you ever been bored with life? And if so, did you ever ask yourself what brought you to be that way?

Svendsen, L. (2005). A philosophy of boredom. Reaktion Books.

183. In any story/book, in your opinion, what are the two most important things that it absolutely must have?

INSIGHTS: If a story didn't have a plot, would you want to read it? More so, could it be called a story if it didn't? Is a story a structure with certain elements?

Storr, W. (2020). The Science of Storytelling: Why Stories Make Us Human and How to Tell Them Better. Abrams.

184. Do you believe that "good things come to those who wait?"

INSIGHTS: Is this true? Or is this just a way to get me out of the way? If I wait too long, then everything will be gone, will it not? Is patience truly the powerful asset that people put it up to be? Or is it just another diversion tactic, making me wait aside so that all the others can swoop in and have their take?

Stevens, J. R., & Stephens, D. W. (2008). Patience.

185. Which people in my life, whether I know them or not, love them or not, are most likely to hold me back from my goals in life?

INSIGHTS: In the crab bucket, who is it that is actually pulling at your feet? Often times the conventional thought on this is that it is you pulling your own feet and hence, yourself back to the bottom of the bucket. However, if we can rule out our own errors and involvement, who is the next likely person who we might find tugging away at us, pulling us back down? And is it always all those random strangers?

Marques, J. (2009). Sisterhood in short supply in the workplace: It's often the women who hold back their female colleagues. Human Resource Management International Digest.

186. Would you say that you have high-expectations for a significant other in a relationship?

INSIGHTS: Can you withstand being disappointed in a relationship? Or does this depend on the nature of the relationship? Does a romantic relationship differ in this way from a typical friendship? Most importantly, where do you stand on all of it?

Fuhrman, R. W., Flannagan, D., & Matamoros, M. (2009). Behavior expectations in cross-sex friendships, same-sex friendships, and romantic relationships. Personal Relationships, 16(4), 575-596.

187. Are you able to sit and think beyond the average level of thoughts?

INSIGHTS: What is it that most people are thinking about most of the time? And is that even knowable at all? If it was, would you say you are thinking about the same things? Or would you say that you think less? Or do you think a little bit more?

Tseng, J., & Poppenk, J. (2020). Brain meta-state transitions demarcate thoughts across task contexts exposing the mental noise of trait neuroticism. Nature communications, 11(1), 1-12.

188. Do you think you would be able to tell if you were going crazy?

INSIGHTS: A crazy person might think you are insane. So, if that is what they would think of you, how would you be able to tell the difference?

Bedford, N. J., & David, A. S. (2014). Denial of illness in schizophrenia as a disturbance of self-reflection, self-perception and insight. Schizophrenia Research, 152(1), 89-96.

189. Why does the human race always end up enabling and empowering tyrants?

INSIGHTS: Why is it that the scum seems to always rise to the top? Better still, why do we step out of the way and, even in some cases, permit and facilitate it? Whether it's us or them, it seems that far too often, we end up with a tyrant in prestigious positions, having control over all. Why is this?

Chirot, D. (1996). Modern tyrants: The power and prevalence of evil in our age. Princeton University Press.

190. How much of what you want is really what you want... ...and how much of what you want came from external subliminal programming?

INSIGHTS: According to certain scholars, brainwashing requires control over all aspects of the subject in question. Given that this is the case, how much of our lives are actually controlled by someone or something? Surely most people would claim they are not controlled whatsoever. However, a quick look at the things that influence us and their prominence in our lives might suggest that we are more out of our own control than we wish to admit.

Taillard, M., & Giscoppa, H. (2013). Brainwashing. In Psychology and Modern Warfare (pp. 73-81). Palgrave Macmillan, New York.

191. How many people consider themselves brainwashed at least some extent, even if it's tiny... and how many people consider themselves truly free?

INSIGHTS: If you were brainwashed by mass media or government, would you be able to tell? Or is the trouble of being brainwashed that you wouldn't be able to tell the difference?

O'Connor, N., & Clark, S. (2019). Beware bandwagons! The bandwagon phenomenon in medicine, psychiatry and management. Australasian Psychiatry, 27(6), 603-606.

192. Is creativity learned or innate?

INSIGHTS: Are we born creative people? Or is this a trait we learn as we go along? Again the nature or nurture debate peaks on through at us and smiles. But what is the real situation here? Did creative people just have a better chance at life? Or do we all have the same capacity of creativity, but that it's just that some are able to manifest their creativity in ways that they get noticed more than others?

Harnad, S. (2006). Creativity: Method or magic? Hungarian Studies, 20(1), 163-177.

193. Besides time and the 3 spatial dimensions, do you think there are other dimensions we can't immediately see 'right in front of us?'

INSIGHTS: Are there just three dimensions of space and one of time? String theory calls for a number, and perhaps there are other theories that might call for more. But are we missing something because of limits on our perception?

Whitrow, G. J. (1955). Why physical space has three dimensions. The British Journal for the Philosophy of Science, 6(21), 13-31.

194. What innovations do you think will come from time crystals?

INSIGHTS: Time crystals are a quantum system that is based on the analogy of the arrangement pattern of atoms in standard crystals. The particles in time crystals, unlike regular crystals, are arranged in time rather than regular crystals, which are arranged in space. Hence, a crystal with all of its particles in its lowest energy state can be made to collectively oscillate in a repetitive motion. As these particles were already in their lowest energy state, they cannot slow up to a stop and lose energy. Thus, time crystals can technically hold a state of perpetual motion.

Wilczek, F. (2012). Quantum time crystals. Physical review letters, 109(16), 160401.

195. What would you do if you lived in the time of a "Mad" Monarch?

INSIGHTS: Nothing like living under the rule of a king who has lost it. How much fun would it be to deal with someone who can immediately do anything they wish to you, including all the gruesome things that went on in dark medieval dungeons.

De Madariaga, I. (2008). Ivan the Terrible. Yale University Press.

196. Why do humans do war?

INSIGHTS: Why war? Why not peace? Why can't we be peaceful? What is war so necessary for? What is it about humans that has left us with a trail of history full of war?

Tooby, J., & Cosmides, L. (1988). The evolution of war and its cognitive foundations. Institute for evolutionary studies technical report, 88(1), 1-15.

197. Do people really believe there are no set-in-stone answers to anything, or is this just a subliminal way to avoid conflict?

INSIGHTS: Is everything in a state of the unknown? Can we ever know anything, or is this just a trick of the human mind? Either way, one thing we do know for sure is that if we don't drink water after a while, that isn't going to end up good.

Audi, R. (2010). Epistemology: A contemporary introduction to the theory of knowledge. Routledge.

198. Is it sound theoretical planning and intuition or serendipity that is responsible for many scientific discoveries?

INSIGHTS: There have been many discoveries made that were not actually in the original script. In fact, many discoveries were the unexpected outcomes of otherwise planned and expected projects. On the other hand, however, scientists have thought up and planned other experiments and had their expected outcomes show up right on time. So is it planning or serendipity that is the real cause for new discoveries?

Copeland, S. (2019). On serendipity in science: discovery at the intersection of chance and wisdom. Synthese, 196(6), 2385-2406.

199. Since we got a number of takes on what an 'alpha-male' is, then what would a 'beta-male' be, in your opinion?

INSIGHTS: What are the differences between these two designations? And more so, which one is the more advantageous one? Although we see the first term thrown around a lot on the internet, what exactly is a beta-male? And why might a beta male exist? And more so, do they exist? Or is this just a misnomer?

Gesquiere, L. R., Learn, N. H., Simao, M. C. M., Onyango, P. O., Alberts, S. C., & Altmann, J. (2011). Life at the top: rank and stress in wild male baboons. Science, 333(6040), 357-360.

200. If you were the world's richest person, would you do it all differently than Jeff Bezos?

INSIGHTS: Jeff Bezos seems to like the idea of space. Others had their eccentric tendencies, habits, and ways. But have you ever thought that in the event you become incredibly wealthy, what would you do, and would it be different than all other wealthy folk before you?

Marcus, G. E. (1995). Three. On eccentricity. In Rhetorics of self-making (pp. 43-58). University of California Press.

201. Why is the deadliest animal, deadly?

INSIGHTS: First off, what is the world's deadliest animal, and then, why is it the deadliest animal? Surely, there are some frightening animals on earth, but which is the worst of them all? And why is that animal so deadly? What does it have above the rest that makes it the deadliest?

Kamerow, D. (2014). The world's deadliest animal. Bmj, 348.

202. Have you ever considered trying out to be a secret agent?

INSIGHTS: Do you have a James Bond gene? Do you think you are cut out to go on secret missions? More so, do you think you could pass the exams and tests that might be required?

West, N. (2020). MI6: British Secret Intelligence Service Operations, 1909–1945. Pen and Sword.

203. Do you find it intriguing that there are many trees on earth which are older than your direct genetic lineage?

INSIGHTS: Although by far not the oldest trees known, one Alerce tree was dated to be 3613 years old. Meanwhile, the AncestryDNA service claims to be able to go back 1000 years using DNA sequencing technology.

Lara, A., & Villalba, R. (1993). A 3620-year temperature record from Fitzroya cupressoides tree rings in southern South America. *Science, 260*(5111), 1104-1106.

https://www.ancestry.com/cs/us/gettingstarted

204. Is it that people need to 'think outside the box,' or 'live outside the box?'

INSIGHTS: Is merely putting your mind outside of your normal train of thoughts enough to really get at a new perspective? Or is it much better to not only think differently but to move into an entirely new environment? Would being immersed in a new environment catalyze a different line of thinking altogether? Or would it just be a waste of time and resources for something that could be done right out of your own head?

Glăveanu, V. P. (2014). Distributed creativity: Thinking outside the box of the creative individual.   Cham/Heidelberger: Springer International Publishing.

205. Are you a personality that everyone can get along with?

INSIGHTS: Although it seems to get much publicity, the Dark Triad does not exist without a counterpart. Indeed, the "Light Triad" focuses on things like having an inner sense of duty to truth, bestowing dignity and respect to all individuals, and believing in people and humanity. The big question to yourself then, would be "Do you tend to lean towards the qualities of the dark or the light?"

Kaufman, S. B., Yaden, D. B., Hyde, E., & Tsukayama, E. (2019). The light vs. dark triad of personality: Contrasting two very different profiles of human nature. Frontiers in psychology, 10, 467.

206. Have you ever had an addiction that you were able to get out of?

INSIGHTS: Addiction is no easy thing to break free from. Many substances and their victims over time are a testament to the hardship and difficulty one faces when under the spell of addiction. Thus, the strength and perseverance one must have to escape and overcome an addiction is likely as close to superhuman as it gets. Thus, did you ever totally escape the clutches of addiction?

Barnes, D. M. (1988). Breaking the cycle of addiction. Science, 241(4869), 1029-1031.

207. Do you think it's possible that anyone could fall victim to Munchausen syndrome?

INSIGHTS: Munchausen syndrome is when someone tries to get attention and sympathy by faking an illness. They will even go to the extent of sabotaging medical tests to validate their case. Of course, as it is defined, this is the case where someone has the intent to do this. But what if someone unknowingly did this to themselves, with no malicious intentions behind them? Could someone who is a hypochondriac unintentionally induce themselves into a similar syndrome? Even worse is Munchausen syndrome by proxy, where a parent or caregiver could be the instigating force.

Meadow, R. (1982). Munchausen syndrome by proxy. Archives of disease in childhood, 57(2), 92-98.

208. Many cultures, independent of one another, have built pyramids. Why pyramids?

INSIGHTS: Why pyramids? But also, while we're at it, why build pyramids where they have built pyramids? Is it because it was easier to build structures in a pyramidal shape, given the construction constraints at the time? But also, how did they know that the sites they selected would still be good all the time after?

Morsy, S. W., & Halim, M. A. (2015). Reasons why the great pyramids of Giza remain the only surviving wonder of the ancient world: drawing ideas from the structure of the Giza pyramids to nuclear power plants. Journal of Civil Engineering and Architecture, 9, 1191-1201.

209. Do you know what the difference between old engine oil (I.e., needs to be changed) and new engine oil is?

INSIGHTS: New   oil   has   appropriate lubricating properties, whereas old oil is lacking in this regard. Thus, the regular oil change is an irreplaceable strategy to restore this component of the vehicle's lubricating system. But the thing is, what happens exactly, that makes engine oil 'old?'

Levermore, D. M., Josowicz, M., Rees, W. S., & Janata, J. (2001). Headspace analysis of engine oil by gas chromatography/mass spectrometry. Analytical chemistry, 73(6), 1361-1365.

210. Can we say that overthinkers are more prone to anxiety and panic attacks?

INSIGHTS: Although it might be a popular suggestion, no studies with both "overthinking" and "panic attacks" in the title seem to come up in current literature searches. Thus, although the association is widely assumed to have some degree of truth, it remains to be shown via testing and with independent groups. Thus, is it really overthinking that is the true catalyst, or do the victims have something else at work that they are unaware of?

Story, M. P. 'Prone to Panic and Accustomed to Anxiety' by Jocelyn Cunningham.

211. Is evolution/change always good?

INSIGHTS: Science is thought to have advanced progress by replacing superstition and erroneous belief with evidence-based testing and conclusion. And along with progress that is welcomed is not only scientific progress but also social and economic progress. Thus, we need to ask, "Is there any type of progress that is bad, besides the progress of an infection?" As there are things that are beneficial, what are some things that may progress or evolve but do not lead to desirable outcomes?

Golinski, J. (2008). Making Natural Knowledge: Constructivism and the History of Science, with a new preface. University of Chicago Press.

212. Do you think we have actually 'lost' technology secrets, that might put us ahead even now, from history's empires and times now long past?

INSIGHTS: Although many advances have come with the modern era, Roman architecture and especially Roman concrete could be said to be still relevant even today. Although the general formula for Roman concrete is known, the fact that many of the structures made with this ancient formulation are still standing is evidence that the Romans were notable innovators. Thus, besides Roman concrete, are there any other innovations from the past that you can think of that might be lost to history?

Jackson, M. D., Mulcahy, S. R., Chen, H., Li, Y., Li, Q., Cappelletti, P., & Wenk, H. R. (2017). Phillipsite and Al-tobermorite mineral cements produced through low-temperature water-rock reactions in Roman marine

concrete. American Mineralogist: Journal of Earth and Planetary Materials, 102(7), 1435-1450.

Delatte, N. J. (2001). Lessons from Roman cement and concrete. Journal of professional issues in engineering education and practice, 127(3), 109-115.

213. Were you born a 'traveler,' or did you become one as you grew up?

INSIGHTS: Some people love to travel, some people don't. But why is this? Are we born this way, or do we pick this up from our parents and the people who influence us? What is it about going somewhere else that is so intriguing to some people? And why do certain people thrive with it while others couldn't be convinced to leave their hometown?

Csikszentmihalyi, M., & Coffey, J. (2016). Why do we travel? A positive psychological model for travel motivation. In Positive tourism (pp. 136-146). Routledge.

214. What do you think is the origin and original reason our species adorns itself with makeup, body modifications, and jewelry?

INSIGHTS: Most often, people will gravitate towards status and beautification when asked this question. Although this is not wrong, it is not the only reason. This behavior goes way back for humans, and it is even thought that Neanderthals might have even done these things as well. It is thought that the ability to do these things draws a line between humans and animals, although one must wonder where that notion first came up.

DeMello, M. (2011). Blurring the divide: Human and animal body modification. A companion to the anthropology of the body and embodiment, 338-352.

215. For those affected: Have you ever reasoned with yourself about why you get imposter syndrome?

INSIGHTS: Impostor Syndrome is defined by the Collins Dictionary as "If you have impostor syndrome, you feel that you do not deserve your status or success." In the article "Imposter Syndrome: Treat the Cause, Not the Symptom," the authors define it as "*Imposter syndrome* is a psychological term that refers to a pattern of behavior wherein people (even those with adequate external evidence of success) doubt their abilities and have a persistent fear of being exposed as a fraud."

Mullangi, S., & Jagsi, R. (2019). Imposter syndrome: treat the cause, not the symptom. Jama, 322(5), 403-404.

https://www.collinsdictionary.com/us/dictio nary/english/impostor-syndrome

216. Can we agree there is a sort of evolutionary sixth sense emerging in some of us that rings the bell and raises the flag when in the proximity to predatorial types?

INSIGHTS: Do we really know a 'bad guy' when we see one? And if so, is this an evolutionarily programmed trait? Have we been programmed to get an uneasy feeling even in the absence of logical cues when in the company of the nefarious? Or is all this just wishful thinking and the imposing of our prejudice on people who may otherwise be good people with solid reputations?

Nado, J. (2014). Why intuition? Philosophy

and Phenomenological Research, 89(1), 15-41.

217. Is reality TV beneficial, or does it have no effect, or is it detrimental?

INSIGHTS: Is reality TV the futures best possible evolution of TV? Is the content covered the most stimulating? Or has quality taken a hit and brought us reality TV? And if it is not the best thing since sliced bread, could it have detrimental effects?

Gibson, B., Thompson, J., Hou, B., & Bushman, B. J. (2016). Just "harmless entertainment"? Effects of surveillance reality TV on physical aggression. Psychology of Popular Media Culture, 5(1), 66.

218. Should anyone else have a say over your body?

INSIGHTS: "Oh yeah, they don't really need that finger; cut it off!" Would you really want someone having that kind of power over your body just because some insane government would legitimize a law to permit something like this?

Herring, J., & Chau, P. L. (2007). My body, your body, our bodies. Medical Law Review, 15(1), 34-61.

219. Is it healthy to have regrets?

INSIGHTS: Is it best to go through life with no regrets? Or is it better to be able to look back and examine whether you were at your best or not? And if so, could you have done things better? Or should you have done things another way?

Baum, S. K. (1999). Who has no regrets? Psychological reports, 85(1), 257-260.

220. Has money made the human experience better or worse or otherwise?

INSIGHTS: Has money made things better for everyone? Or has it only made things better for a few? Or is money simply a misunderstood representation that keeps getting a bad reputation? Either way, will money eventually come to make everyone's lives better?

Diener, E., & Biswas-Diener, R. (2002). Will

money increase subjective well-being? Social indicators research, 57(2), 119-169.

221. What was the greatest scam ever?

INSIGHTS: Are the scams that are advertised in the news the only scams? Or are we fooled in the sense that we only let the media judge what a scam is? How do you not know that the things around you every day are not scams? What is your proof?

Henriques, D. B. (2018). A case study of a con man: Bernie Madoff and the timeless lessons of history's biggest Ponzi scheme. Social Research: An International Quarterly, 85(4), 745-766.

222. Can you say you understand the concepts of 'signal' and 'noise?'

INSIGHTS: When you are in a conversation, can you tell which parts are signal and which parts are noise? Likewise, when you listen to TV, can you tell which parts are signal and which parts are noise?

Woodward, J. (2010). Data, phenomena,

signal, and noise. Philosophy of Science, 77(5), 792-803.

223. Is our system made the way the elites want it, or is it the way the greater populace wants it?

INSIGHTS: So who is really behind the whole 9 to 5? Is it the elite overlords? Or is it the people themselves, all rushing into the point where things equilibrate out to a 40-hour workweek as that is what most people are willing to do?

Costas, J., & Grey, C. (2012). Outsourcing your Life: Exploitation and Exploration in "the 4-Hour Workweek". In Managing 'Human Resources' by Exploiting and Exploring People's Potentials. Emerald Group Publishing Limited.

224. Did the internet change people, or just reveal who we really are?

INSIGHTS: Did the internet chance humans? Or did the internet finally pull back the curtain on how people really are? Or does the internet's anonymity take away certain inhibitions that were there before?

Loh, K. K., & Kanai, R. (2016). How has the Internet reshaped human cognition?. The Neuroscientist, 22(5), 506-520.

225. What is more advantageous, being a deep thinker, or being an overthinker?

INSIGHTS: Is overthinking just pathological? Or is it a noisy and expensive way of generating random answers? Or is this deep thinking? Does deep thinking use a better method for thinking about the issues we face? Or are these both one and the same?

Vangkilde, K. T., & Sausdal, D. B. (2016, May). Overponderabilia: Overcoming Overthinking When Studying" Ourselves". In Forum Qualitative Sozialforschung/Forum: Qualitative Social Research (Vol. 17, No. 2).

226. Do you think that 'Zombies' are possible?

INSIGHTS: Is it all just a bunch of overhyped fiction? Or is it possible that Zombies could exist? As certain parts of the world do indeed believe they are able to create zombies, have you ever wondered if this is just fiction? Or is it true?

Kirk, R. (2007). Zombies and consciousness. Oxford University Press.

227. Do you think it is possible to make an animal biology textbook/course about human behavior that is accurate?

INSIGHTS: Is animal behavior the same as human behavior? Or is this untrue? And if it is untrue, what differences between animals and humans compel you to say this?

Povinelli, D. J., & Vonk, J. (2003). Chimpanzee minds: suspiciously human? Trends in cognitive sciences, 7(4), 157-160.

228. Are you able to force yourself to get along with someone who you definitely don't get along with?

INSIGHTS: Can you smile and nod it all off? Or are you counting the seconds till you can stand it anymore? Are there personalities that you just clash with? And if so, why is this the case?

Gignac, G. E., & Callis, Z. M. (2020). The costs of being exceptionally intelligent:

Compatibility and interpersonal skill concerns. Intelligence, 81, 101465.

229. Can all conspiracy theories be completely written off?

INSIGHTS: As crazy as they all may seem, is it possible that at least a few may have some degree of truth to them? Or is this just giving the benefit of the doubt where it shouldn't be given? Are these crazy tales all just simply rumors that are made up to get someone's personal attention?

Pelkmans, M., & Machold, R. (2011). Conspiracy theories and their truth trajectories. Focaal, 2011(59), 66-80.

230. Have humans figured anything out at all?

INSIGHTS: If the truth deniers out there are correct, we likely won't know anything and hence, don't have anything figured out. But is this true given how many things we know how to use and manipulate? All those computers and vehicles out there must be an indication that we got at least something figured out, true?

Zeldin, T. (2012). An intimate history of humanity. Random House.

231. In an afterlife, would you be the same age as you were at the time of death?

INSIGHTS: When we hit the afterlife, what kind of shape are we in? Are we the prime version of who we were? Or are we as we were when we died? And what about those unfortunate folks who never make it to their prime? Do we find them in their prime as it would have been? And how would we recognize everyone if they weren't the same as they were when we knew them?

Bremmer, J. N. (2003). The rise and fall of the afterlife. Routledge.

232. Does meditation work?

INSIGHTS: Although it might give us a moment of quiet, does meditation give us anything more? Or is this just a great way to get a much needed time out from the insanity of modern life?

Manocha, R. (2000). Why meditation?

Australian Family Physician, 29(12), 1135-1138.

233. What is time?

INSIGHTS: Is time really what we perceive it to be? Or is what we perceive just simply a tiny fraction of what it really is in the objective sense?

Newton-Smith, W. H. (2018). The structure of time. Routledge.

234. Do you think self-made people are really so self-made, given the interconnectedness of our society?

INSIGHTS: Are those who claim to be self-made really so self-made in the true sense of the term? After all, they might have worked hard, but they drove on roads to get to work that others designed, paved, and maintained, among other things. So are they really self-made?

Catano, J. V. (2001). Ragged dicks: Masculinity, steel, and the rhetoric of the self-made man. SIU Press.

235. Do you believe in charity donation?

INSIGHTS: Do you believe you are doing good things when you donate money to charity? And does that charity send your money to the right places? Or is that money going where you think it is? What if it isn't? How would you really know the difference?

Lee, Y. K., & Chang, C. T. (2007). Who gives what to charity? Characteristics affecting donation behavior. Social Behavior and Personality: an international journal, 35(9), 1173-1180.

236. What do you consider to be true 'intelligence?'

INSIGHTS: The word 'intelligence' gets thrown around a lot. Despite how it is used in common use, what does it really mean? Obviously, it doesn't mean 'stupid,' but what is true intelligence? Is there really such a thing?

Sternberg, R. J. (2013). Intelligence. John Wiley & Sons, Inc.

237. Do you consider yourself a graduate of the school of 'hard knocks?'

INSIGHTS: Did you have to do life the hard way? Did you start all the way from the bottom and work your way to the top? Or did you have it all given to you? Still, even if you got it all given to you, did you still have a tough time navigating through all of life's many hurdles?

Chetty, R., Friedman, J. N., Hendren, N., Jones, M. R., & Porter, S. R. (2018). The opportunity atlas: Mapping the childhood roots of social mobility (No. w25147). National Bureau of Economic Research.

238. What do you think made people choose a major religion over any alternatives?

INSIGHTS: Given how many people have personal beliefs and spiritualities, why did so many end up joining the mainstream? Like, what is the benefit of believing in the same things as everyone else?

Ben-Jochannan, Y. (1991). African Origins of the Major" Western Religions" (Vol. 1). Black Classic Press.

239. Why is Jesus not written about with expected volume and respect in contemporaneous Roman texts?

INSIGHTS: We got a whole bible complete with four individual takes on Jesus, but why is the bible the only book with these detailed accounts on the life of Jesus coming from around that time? Why are the Romans not writing so extensively about a guy who was supposedly nothing less than miraculous?

Lataster, R. C. (2015). Jesus Did Not Exist: A Debate among Atheists. Raphael C. Lataster.

240. In observing quantum mechanical experiments, do you think its possible the observer observing these experiments might be leading to misleading experimental results?

INSIGHTS: Is the observer skewing or influencing the results of quantum experiments? If so, how? If not, how do you know if that is true?

Stapp, H. P. (2011). Mindful universe: Quantum mechanics and the participating observer. Springer Science & Business Media.

241. When you make a guess or a call on something, how often do you find that you are correct?

INSIGHTS: Are you always on point with your guesses? If so, why do you think that might be? Also, do you challenge yourself across all possible scenarios? Or do you just restrict yourself to the familiar ones?

Dunning, D. (2011). The Dunning–Kruger effect: On being ignorant of one's own ignorance. In Advances in experimental social psychology (Vol. 44, pp. 247-296). Academic Press.

242. Is someone who takes regular selfies highly probable to be a narcissist?

INSIGHTS: Is taking numerous selfies narcissistic? Or is it just being overplayed as narcissistic? How does this translate to someone being a complete narcissist?

Taylor, D. G. (2020). Putting the "self" in selfies: how narcissism, envy and self-promotion motivate sharing of travel photos through social media. Journal of Travel & Tourism Marketing, 37(1), 64-77.

243. Do you believe someone can be overeducated?

INSIGHTS: Some people claim that people can know too much. Other people claim that we can't know enough. So which one is it? And since when is the job market the great knower and seer of all things? Can someone be truly overeducated?

Verhaest, D., & Omey, E. (2006). The impact of overeducation and its measurement. Social Indicators Research, 77(3), 419-448.

244. What, to you, defines a true victim?

INSIGHTS: Many people claim to be a victim of one thing or another. But who is a real victim and who is someone just trying to avoid placing blame on themselves? Surely there are real victims, but is it possible that some others might not be?

Chouliaraki, L., & Banet-Weiser, S. (2021). Introduction to special issue: The logic of victimhood.

245. Do you believe we came from a primordial muck supplemented with asteroid collisions?

INSIGHTS: Is it possible that we came from an aqueous environment in the depth of the oceans? And could this all have been spiced up with asteroid collisions, providing not only other molecules but also high energy situations that might have been conducive to the formation of supramolecular structures?

Daniel, I., Oger, P., & Winter, R. (2006). Origins of life and biochemistry under high-pressure conditions. Chemical Society Reviews, 35(10), 858-875.

246. Has there ever been anyone with true, tested and verified psychic powers?

INSIGHTS: Did anyone ever take James Randi's offer of $10,000 USD for a demonstration of true psychic powers? Has there ever been anyone who has been able to repeatedly and perfectly demonstrate any psychic powers?

Alcock, J. E. (1987). Parapsychology: Science of the anomalous or search for the soul? Behavioral and Brain Sciences, 10(4), 553-565.

247. Do you believe that what goes around comes around?

INSIGHTS: Do the bad guys really win in the end? Or do they actually lose? Is there some anthropocentric force out there that doles out justice? Or does history indicate otherwise?

White, C. J., Norenzayan, A., & Schaller, M. (2019). The content and correlates of belief in Karma across cultures. Personality and Social Psychology Bulletin, 45(8), 1184-1201.

248. Do you ever think they will be able to perfectly unfry an egg?

INSIGHTS: Unfry, that is, in a way that does not involve a chemical dissolving process or other such treatment. Like, how can we unfry an egg such that we bring it back to where it is just like it was when it was freshly cracked in the frying pan?

Cassirer, E. (1969). Interdisciplinary Perspectives of Time.

249. Do you consider yourself streetsmart or booksmart?

INSIGHTS: Which one would you say you are?   Did you grow up learning from the circumstances of your life and your environment? Or did you get wise from reading books and studying?

Curry, D. S. (2020). Street smarts. Synthese, 1-20.

250. Do you ever think you could have been started off on the wrong advice?

INSIGHTS: Is all advice good?   And is all advice good for you?   Even if it comes from someone who might be a great mind, is that advice in any way relevant to you and your life? How would you know if what people are telling you could have been the best possible thing to tell you?

Levine, S. S., & Prietula, M. (2020). When Advice Can Harm. In Academy of Management Proceedings (Vol. 2020, No. 1, p. 12331). Briarcliff Manor, NY 10510: Academy of Management.

251. Do dreams come from pieces of real life, or from somewhere else?

INSIGHTS: Are we tapping into another, parallel dimension when we dream? Or is it just a bunch of our memories that are being played out of sequence in an odd order?

Domhoff, G. W. (2003). The scientific study of dreams: Neural networks, cognitive development, and content analysis. American Psychological Association.

252. Would you rather be educated or entertained?

INSIGHTS: Is education overrated? Like, if there is a cap on how much humans can learn, then why bother? Why not just spend our lives in sweet, ignorant bliss? Why would someone want to learn anything when we might be better off just having fun?

Killeen, F. (1953). Bread and Circuses. Journal of the Galway Archaeological and Historical Society, 25(3/4), 67-77.

253. Have you ever been surrounded by frenemies?

INSIGHTS: Are your friends really your friends? Or are there certain behaviors that just seem too odd to be coming from people who supposedly have your best interests in mind? Do your friends really want the best for you? Or do you have a feeling that they might actually be imposters who just happen to have front-row seats to your demise?

Wójcik, M., & Flak, W. (2019). Frenemy: A new addition to the bullying circle. Journal of interpersonal violence, 0886260519880168.

254. Is it interest or ability that determines one's true capacity?

INSIGHTS: Can I reach the top on motivation alone? Or do I need to be born for that sort of thing? What is the real force at work here?

Canning, E. A., Muenks, K., Green, D. J., & Murphy, M. C. (2019). STEM faculty who believe ability is fixed have larger racial achievement gaps and inspire less student motivation in their classes. Science advances, 5(2), eaau4734.

255. Could life have no meaning?

INSIGHTS: People don't like to hear it. And they don't like to hear about it to the extent that it could cause a ruckus. No one want's to hear the nihilist's point of view, but is it possible that this could actually be the situation?

Tartaglia, J. (2016). Philosophy in a meaningless life: A system of nihilism, consciousness and reality. Bloomsbury Academic.

256. Do all religions and spiritualities worship the same deity?

INSIGHTS: Is it *this* God? Or is it *that* God? Who's God is it? If there is only one God, then who are the other people praying to? Or is it a case where different religions are different channels to God? Either way, is it possible to sort out this confusion?

Goshen-Gottstein, A. (2012). God Between Christians and Jews: Is It the Same God? Do We Worship the Same God? Jews, Christians, and Muslims in Dialogue, 50-75.

257. Can people accurately assess their own intelligence?

INSIGHTS: Can a person truly and accurately know their own intelligence level? If so, how so? How can they assess this in an unbiased way? Or is this even possible at all?

Furnham, A., & Chamorro-Premuzic, T. (2004). Estimating one's own personality and intelligence scores. British Journal of Psychology, 95(2), 149-160.

258. How many people do you think are currently affected by social anxiety?

INSIGHTS: A lot of people seem to have anxiety. But then, it's almost like our world doesn't believe that there are *that* many people that could be affected. So, how many people would you say are affected by regular anxiety?

Fehm, L., Beesdo, K., Jacobi, F., & Fiedler, A. (2008). Social anxiety disorder above and below the diagnostic threshold: prevalence, comorbidity and impairment in the general population. Social psychiatry and psychiatric epidemiology, 43(4), 257-265.

259. Which animals besides humans are religious?

INSIGHTS: Where is the feline house of worship? Or the canine ministries? Although it might not be on that scale, is it possible that animals have religion just like humans do? And if so, why would they have this same behavior as humans do?

Siegel, R. K. (1977). Religious behavior in animals and man: drug-induced effects. Journal of Drug Issues, 7(3), 219-236.

260. How much corruption actually goes on?

INSIGHTS: Is everything in the world totally honest? I doubt anyone will agree with that statement. So, as this is the case, what is the degree of corruption that actually goes on? But then we have to ask, would we even be able to measure such a thing as, after all, corruption usually doesn't like being figured out.

Johnson, R. (2004). The struggle against corruption: A comparative study. Springer.

261. Why do humans find what they find terrifying, terrifying?

INSIGHTS: Why are certain things scary and other things are not? What makes something scary to people, whereas other things are not?

Öhman, A. (2009). Of snakes and faces: An evolutionary perspective on the psychology of fear. Scandinavian journal of psychology, 50(6), 543-552.

Öhman, A., Carlsson, K., Lundqvist, D., & Ingvar, M. (2007). On the unconscious subcortical origin of human fear. Physiology & behavior, 92(1-2), 180-185.

262. Is filial piety always the best path?

INSIGHTS: Are all parents always good? But what can we say about a scenario where one's parents may not have one's best intentions in mind?

Yeh, K. H. (2003). The beneficial and harmful effects of filial piety: An integrative analysis. Progress in Asian Social Psychology: Conceptual and Empirical Contributions: Conceptual and Empirical Contributions, 42, 67-82.

263. Are humans best suited for individualism, tribalism, or collectivism?

INSIGHTS: Can everyone be their own, distinct person? Or do we find our tribe, a collection of people who are very similar to us but who also have differences from the rest? Or are we just like everyone else? Whichever scenario seems more plausible, the question is, which one really suits you the best?

Santos, H. C., Varnum, M. E., & Grossmann, I. (2017). Global increases in individualism. Psychological science, 28(9), 1228-1239.

264. Is the hard problem of consciousness actually 'hard?'

INSIGHTS: Is the hard problem of consciousness really hard? Or are we overcomplicating it? More so, are we adding in too much detail? Or are we subtracting too much away from it? More so, has everyone read all the literature on neuroscience and psychology that exists?

Melloni, L., Mudrik, L., Pitts, M., & Koch, C. (2021). Making the hard problem of consciousness easier. Science, 372(6545), 911-912.

265. Is there an afterlife?

INSIGHTS: Humans have believed, thought about, wondered, and even doubted the existence of an afterlife, likely for quite some time. But the thing is, does an afterlife exist? If so, how are we able to prove this? Most often, however, no one is able to either prove it or disprove it, so such a thing seems to rest on faith alone.

Andrade, G. (2011). Immortality.

266. Why are monsters scary just by appearance alone?

INSIGHTS: Are all monsters scary? Or are some not? Is there a form that is always scary? Or does it vary from person to person? And even if it does, what is the general form of monster that we can all agree on that would be 'scary?'

Tattersall, I. (2000). Once we were not alone. Scientific American, 282(1), 56-62.

267. Do all questions have a correct answer?

INSIGHTS: Is it true that there is a correct answer to every question that one can come up with? Or is it that there are questions that may be unanswerable?

Turnbull, N. (2008). Dewey's philosophy of questioning: science, practical reason and democracy. History of the Human Sciences, 21(1), 49-75.

268. Is being good at school equivalent to intelligence?

INSIGHTS: There is school, and then there is real life. Are these two things the same? Or is there a big difference between how well one does in school versus how well one does in the real world?

Gardner, H. (1999). Who owns intelligence. The Atlantic Monthly, 283(2), 67-76.

269. What started anti-intellectualism?

INSIGHTS: What is so appealing about not knowing things? And more so, what is so appealing about looking down on those that do know things and think? Given that humanity went through some surely difficult times during its existence, the power of knowledge always seems to be an advantage.

Rigney, D. (1991). Three kinds of anti-intellectualism: Rethinking Hofstadter. Sociological Inquiry, 61(4), 434-451.

270. Should political correctness be made law?

INSIGHTS: If people continue to be marginalized, then why not erase it all by making political correctness law? Why not have people fined or jailed should they utter something offensive? If marginalization still exists and can be ameliorated by enforcing political correctness, why not just go ahead and do it? It seems that the counter-arguments are an infringement on free speech and setting boundaries as to what actually constitutes 'bad' speech versus 'correct' speech. Either way, will political correctness help achieve equality for all?

Ford, B. R. (2017). Political correctness. In Oxford Research Encyclopedia of Communication.

271. Will marriage come to an end soon?

INSIGHTS: With all those rules and the legal system making such a union a potential disaster hanging from a cliff edge, is it really so wise to walk into a marriage in modern times? Sure it's all about the kids, but is it really? It's more like "Three easy steps to effectively dissolve a family and all their happiness in one shot" once things hit the courtroom.

Furstenberg, F. F. (2015). Will marriage disappear? Proceedings of the American Philosophical Society, 159(3), 241-246.

272. What gets in your way the most in life?

INSIGHTS: Is it really always you that gets in your own way in life? It is always ourselves that we have to solely blame when things don't work out or go our way? And who is the one that tells us this? After all, if one has no access to resources, then how could one do something that would mandatorily require the use of such resources?

Lucas, J. R. (1995). Responsibility.

273. How much of your life was purely decided on your own ideas and terms?

INSIGHTS: Do all the things we do come from our own wants? Or did other people just direct us towards them? Who set what we are supposed to do, and are we really even supposed to be doing exactly that?

Marmor, A. (2009). Social conventions. Princeton University Press.

274. Do you think you have ever been in the presence of a potential serial killer?

INSIGHTS: If you've ever been in a crowd, there is a chance there was a few potential serial killers standing in that same crowd. Have you ever wondered who they might have been?

Allely, C. S., Minnis, H., Thompson, L., Wilson, P., & Gillberg, C. (2014). Neurodevelopmental and psychosocial risk factors in serial killers and mass murderers. Aggression and violent behavior, 19(3), 288-301.

275. Do you think you are misunderstood?

INSIGHTS: Does anyone get you? Do they get what you say? Do you always feel as if they never quite grasp what it is you are trying to say? And is this not just with one or a few people, but with everyone you run into? What could possibly be the reason for this? And more so, is it them? Or is it something about you?

Lun, J., Kesebir, S., & Oishi, S. (2008). On feeling understood and feeling well: The role of interdependence. Journal of Research in Personality, 42(6), 1623-1628.

276. How will quantum computers change things?

INSIGHTS: If Windows 95' and the internet brought about changes, what would something as powerful as a personal quantum computer be able to do? Of course, none of us are fortune tellers, but given that we've already seen what the internet has done, what changes do you think might accompany quantum computers?

De Wolf, R. (2017). The potential impact of quantum computers on society. Ethics and Information Technology, 19(4), 271-276.

277. Why can't most people, right now, outrun Usain Bolt?

INSIGHTS: Why are some people better at things than others? Do the genetically gifted always have a significant edge over the rest? More so, could someone possibly be missing out on their genetic strengths? Or is it that only some people have some and most others don't have any?

Ahmetov, I. I., & Rogozkin, V. A. (2009). Genes, athlete status and training–An overview. Genetics and sports, 54, 43-71.

278. What will be the next species of the homo genus?

INSIGHTS: What kind of change will bring about the next species after H. sapiens? What could possibly confer the next species an advantage over H. sapiens such that it might come to be dominant in time?

Crow, T. J. (2000). Schizophrenia as the price that Homo sapiens pays for language: a resolution of the central paradox in the origin of the species. Brain research reviews, 31(2-3), 118-129.

279. How do you know that you can be certain on a given statement or topic?

INSIGHTS: Are we sure that what we're saying actually checks out? Are we sure that we know that what we are claiming actually holds in reality? Or are we just saying things that have been said before but haven't been properly checked and put to the test?

Wittgenstein, L., Anscombe, G. E. M., von Wright, G. H., Paul, D., & Anscombe, G. E. M. (1969). On certainty (Vol. 174). Oxford: Blackwell.

280. How long did it take for you to believe in yourself?

INSIGHTS: Have you gotten to the point in your life where you truly believe in yourself? How do you know? What makes you so sure? Either way, if you do, how long did it take for you to get there?

Bénabou, R., & Tirole, J. (2002). Self-confidence and personal motivation. The quarterly journal of economics, 117(3), 871-915.

281. Why do humans like games?

INSIGHTS: We take it for granted, but what is so alluring about games? The fate of a person's day can entirely be based on whether or not their team won or not. And if it isn't hanging off the TV or yelling out loud in the stadium, people like games of all sorts. So, what is it about games that have H. sapiens so hypnotized?

Hamari, J., & Keronen, L. (2017). Why do people play games? A meta-analysis. International Journal of Information Management, 37(3), 125-141.

282. Have you ever tried to invent something?

INSIGHTS: Have you actually ever tried to invent something? What made you decided to do so? Or on the other hand, what made you decide not to do so? Is inventing a healthy pastime? And if you did ever get anything, did you look into how you might patent it?

Shane, S. A. (1992). Why do some societies invent more than others? Journal of Business Venturing, 7(1), 29-46.

283. Why do scam artists still exist?

INSIGHTS: Is there really a sucker born every minute? Are people truly foolish? If the same tricks can be played over and over, what does this say about H. sapiens? Are we just gullible creatures? Or is there more to the story?

Mercier, H. (2017). How gullible are we? A review of the evidence from psychology and social science. Review of General Psychology, 21(2), 103-122.

284. Why do people like averages and first place winners?

INSIGHTS: What is it about simplifying things that seems to go so well with the human brain?

Maguire, P., Moser, P., & Maguire, R. (2016). Understanding consciousness as data compression. Journal of Cognitive Science, 17(1), 63-94.

Bates, C. J., & Jacobs, R. A. (2020). Efficient data compression in perception and perceptual memory. Psychological review, 127(5), 891.

285. Do you think it is possible that each day we wake up into a new dimensional reality?

INSIGHTS: Do we branch off into a new universe every second? Does our experience continue on one possible path while others move on in different dimensions? Or do we just exist in a singular 'life-dimension?'

Byrne, P. (2007). The many worlds of Hugh Everett. Scientific American, 297(6), 98-105.

286. Is someone that is able to make a lot of friends a talented person?

INSIGHTS: Is making friends a talent? Or is making friends not such a 'superficial' endeavor? But there are people who seem to be better than others at making friends. But is this friendship true friendship? Or is it shallow?

Lease, A. M., Kennedy, C. A., & Axelrod, J. L. (2002). Children's social constructions of popularity. Social development, 11(1), 87-109.

287. Has humanity become too materialistic?

INSIGHTS: Do we race to buy too much? Is this something we want to do, or is there really no other alternative? What is it that compels us to race for material goods and dedicate a great portion of our lives to doing this? Is materialism the answer for H. sapiens?

Dittmar, H. (2005). Compulsive buying–a growing concern? An examination of gender, age, and endorsement of materialistic values as predictors. British journal of psychology, 96(4), 467-491.

288. How do you think traffic jams affect people's mental health?

INSIGHTS: Traffic jams can't be good, right? Or is it that they have no effect? Or are they good, and we just don't register it?

Nadrian, H., Taghdisi, M. H., Pouyesh, K., Khazaee-Pool, M., & Babazadeh, T. (2019). "I am sick and tired of this congestion": perceptions of Sanandaj inhabitants on the family mental health impacts of urban traffic jam. Journal of Transport & Health, 14, 100587.

289. Do memory puzzles actually increase/enhance memory?

INSIGHTS: Are memory puzzles definitely good for increasing/enhancing mental health? Or is this just what the companies want you to think?

Luca, S., Nauert, E., Chichester, K., Buckner, J., Foo, P., & Kaur, A. W. (2017). Working memory and cognitive flexibility training reveals no relationship to fluid intelligence in college students. IMPULSE: The Premier Undergraduate Neuroscience Journal, 1-10.

290. Why are lifeforms composed of cells?

INSIGHTS: Why, of all things, is life composed of cells? Like, why is the cell the unit of life? Why couldn't it have been something else? Why couldn't it have been composed without cells? What is it that made life be constructed with cells?

Zwart, H. (2019). Philosophy of Biology: From primal scenes to synthetic cells. Elife, 8, e46518.

291. How much of life is actually fun?

INSIGHTS: Is every minute of life the best fun you've ever had? Also, are there parts of life that tend to stand out as being more fun than others? Or is it that fun is a rarity, something that only comes around occasionally?

Podilchak, W. (1991). Distinctions of fun, enjoyment and leisure. Leisure studies, 10(2), 133-148.

292. Do you think you can manifest your wishes?

INSIGHTS: If you believe hard enough and you concentrate hard enough, do you think you can get what you want to actually come into reality? Or is this just coincidence-based and all of it all just an illusion perpetuated by your mind?

Von Hippel, W., & Trivers, R. (2011). The evolution and psychology of self-deception. Behavioral and brain sciences, 34(1), 1.

293. Given we are highly social creatures, is it cruel to ostracize or leave out other human beings?

INSIGHTS: Is leaving people out as bad as bullying? Given that it seems that humans seek company, are we being cruel when we leave people out?

Van Beest, I., & Williams, K. D. (2006). When inclusion costs and ostracism pays, ostracism still hurts. Journal of personality and social psychology, 91(5), 918.

294. Is humanity's biggest creation the human population?

INSIGHTS: Is it the microchip or the life support unit? Or is humanity's greatest creation humanity? Is it that we are a wonder among animals in that we are able to hyperpopulate the planet yet still maintain a relatively balanced ecology within it? Or is this not the case?

Li, C. N., & Hombert, J. M. (2002). On the evolutionary origin of language. Advances in Consciousness Research, 42, 175-206.

295. Have you ever felt that you were not alone in a house or a room?

INSIGHTS: Do you ever get the feeling you're being watched? Especially when you know you're all alone? Are you really alone? Or is there something else in there too, watching you?

Raihani, N. J., & Bell, V. (2019). An evolutionary perspective on paranoia. Nature human behaviour, 3(2), 114-121.

296. Will we ever be able to time travel?

INSIGHTS: Despite the things said by world-renowned scientists, do you think there is still a chance that we may be able to figure out time travel in the distant future? Do you think humanity will be able to uncover the secrets

Smeenk, C., & Wuthrich, C. (2009). Time travel and time machines.

297. How much perception bias does the average person have?

INSIGHTS: Does the average person have balanced judgment? Or is there a bias somewhere? Or are they completely biased? Or are they on point with their judgments?

Ioannidis, J. P., Munafo, M. R., Fusar-Poli, P., Nosek, B. A., & David, S. P. (2014). Publication and other reporting biases in cognitive sciences: detection, prevalence, and prevention. Trends in cognitive sciences, 18(5), 235-241.

298. Are we a naturally civil species, or are we just acting that way?

INSIGHTS: Is it in our DNA as H. sapiens to be naturally civil and peaceful? Or are we something else? Or, even more so, are we the exact opposite of civil and just act civil when we have too much pressure on us not to be civil? What is the real case with H. sapiens?

Rogan, M. S., Lindsey, P. A., Tambling, C. J., Golabek, K. A., Chase, M. J., Collins, K., & McNutt, J. W. (2017). Illegal bushmeat hunters compete with predators and threaten wild herbivore populations in a global tourism hotspot. Biological Conservation, 210, 233-242.

299. How long until the Amazon rainforest is gone?

INSIGHTS: Do people tend to leave things to the last minute and beyond? Or is this humanity's default move? As the Amazon decreases in size every day, are we all fine with it being hacked down for cash crops and other similar activities? And if so, will that have any impact on the rest of the earth, given the size of the Amazon?

Walt, S. M. (2019). Who will save the Amazon (and how). Foreign Policy, 5.

300. Do you know what the difference is between physics and metaphysics?

INSIGHTS: Can you say you know when you are talking about physics and then metaphysics? Do you understand where the line is drawn between these two fields? What makes something metaphysical, and then what makes something physics?

Vilchis, R. M. (2018). The Distinction Between Physics and Metaphysics in Duhem's Philosophy. Revista Portuguesa de Filosofia, 74(1), 85-114.

301. In your experience, what is the ultimate illusion in life?

INSIGHTS: What is the first thing that you consider an illusion when you think of all things that could be an illusion? Is it just the things that people commonly label as such? Or are the established institutions also fair game for an assessment?

Hayflick, L. (2003). Living forever and dying in the attempt. Experimental gerontology, 38(11-12), 1231-1241.

302. Have we seen evolution happen?

INSIGHTS: Scientists find all sorts of evidence for evolution, but given the long time scale it occurs on, is there any way to see it in a human lifespan? If not elephants, are there any other creatures that we might be able to see it happen with? For which creatures could we see it happen in?

Grant, N. A., Abdel Magid, A., Franklin, J., Dufour, Y., & Lenski, R. E. (2020). Changes in Cell Size and Shape During 50,000 Generations of Experimental Evolution with Escherichia coli. Journal of Bacteriology, 203(10), e00469-20.

303. Do you think everyone is entitled to a home of their own?

INSIGHTS: Should everyone be at least entitled to a home of their own? Or should everyone have to either work for one or inherit one? Given that it helps people to have somewhere to live in order to stay alive, is this something that all people deserve?

Amar, A. R. (1990). Property and the Constitution: Panel II--Forty Acres and a Mule: A Republican Theory of Minimal Entitlements. Harv. JL & Pub. Pol'y, 13, 37.

304. Are you skeptical of things that have big hype behind them?

INSIGHTS: Do you find yourself following the trail of hype? Or do you find yourself more skeptical? Does the trail to hype always lead to beneficial places? Or is it all just a lure to something dressed in bells and whistles that is essentially filled with nothing?

Vasterman, P. L. (2005). Media-hype: Self-reinforcing news waves, journalistic standards and the construction of social problems. European Journal of Communication, 20(4), 508-530.

305. Do you think Shakespeare wrote all his own works?

INSIGHTS: Did Shakespeare write every one of the works that are attributed to him?

Freebury-Jones, D. (2017). Did Shakespeare Really Co-Write 2 Henry VI with Marlowe? ANQ: A Quarterly Journal of Short Articles, Notes and Reviews, 30(3), 137-141.

306. Would you consider getting cryogenically frozen in order to be preserved?

INSIGHTS: Do you wish to be cryogenically preserved and revived one day when science has everything figured out? Or do you believe that it is bogus and that this will never be possible?

Dein, S. (2021). Cryonics: Science or Religion. Journal of Religion and Health, 1-13.

307. Why do we experience pain?

INSIGHTS: Despite the claims that pain may have advantages, to those suffering from it, it certainly doesn't seem so. How does someone in chronic, sharp nauseating pain gain any advantage? And mental pain, too, seems like it has no advantage for the sufferer, seeming more like nature enjoys torment more so than it does the well-being of the sufferer. So why does this exist at all?

McGrath, P. A. (1994). Psychological aspects of pain perception. Archives of Oral Biology, 39, S55-S62.

308. How many humans can live on earth without an issue?

INSIGHTS: So is there a limit? Or is there no limit? Can we expand our population indefinitely? Is this even possible?

Zhang, Y., Wei, Y., & Zhang, J. (2021). Overpopulation and urban sustainable development—population carrying capacity in Shanghai based on probability-satisfaction evaluation method. Environment, Development and Sustainability, 23(3), 3318-3337.

309. Are you in favor of a universal basic income?

INSIGHTS: The job world is far from ideal. Companies only want those that are favored or are brought in by nepotism and cronyism more often than they do seek those who may be truly skilled. Thus, in the whole mess of the job world, many talented people are left out. So what do we do? Leave people hung out to dry all because they aren't the sought out sort that will turn into an ultra-crony? Do people only deserve to be out of poverty if they are employed only? Or is a universal basic income a pipe dream? And most importantly, have we sorted out the problems that might come with a universal basic income?

Van Parijs, P. (2013). The universal basic income: Why utopian thinking matters, and how sociologists can contribute to it. Politics & Society, 41(2), 171-182.

310. Do people really 'fake sick?'

INSIGHTS: Is that a real illness, a misdiagnosis, or is it just fiction? Do people really fake sick? And do they do it in adult life? And if so, why would they do it? Do they hate their job? Do they dislike their situation? What is it that motivates someone to go to the point of faking sick? Or do people fake sick at all? More so, could the pressure or power of managers and bosses be too much for some people to the point that it would make someone fake sick?

Feldman, M. D. (2013). Playing sick? Untangling the web of Munchausen syndrome, Munchausen by proxy, malingering, and factitious disorder. Routledge.

311. Are all humans curious?

INSIGHTS: Is everyone curious? Or are some people just more curious than others? And if so, why are only some people curious and others less so? What would be behind this?

Kobayashi, K., Ravaioli, S., Baranès, A., Woodford, M., & Gottlieb, J. (2019). Diverse motives for human curiosity. Nature human behaviour, 3(6), 587-595.

312. Are innocent bystanders truly 'innocent?'

INSIGHTS: When people just stand around while an atrocity takes place, are they okay in that it isn't their business to interfere? Or are they morally obligated to intervene? And if they are, where is it written that they are to intervene? Are they obligated by natural law to intervene? Or is it just the right thing to do?

Read, J. D., Tollestrup, P., Hammersley, R., McFadzen, E., & Christensen, A. (1990). The unconscious transference effect: Are innocent bystanders ever misidentified? Applied Cognitive Psychology, 4(1), 3-31.

313. Why do people masquerade the exception as the rule?

INSIGHTS: Out of a thousand times, why is it that some folks will jump up to point out the one time something didn't work? And further, why will they then claim that the one instance is the actual case or representation of the phenomenon at hand?

Delgado-Rodriguez, M., & Llorca, J. (2004). Bias. Journal of Epidemiology & Community Health, 58(8), 635-641.

314. If holy books are complete and comprehensive texts, then why do they not have quantum mechanics clearly outlined and included in the content?

INSIGHTS: First of all, when did people start calling quantum mechanics, quantum mechanics? The whole idea must have started somewhere, given that quantum mechanics is a theory. And if it has been around for so long, why didn't the Romans or the Greeks have the Schrodinger equation inscribed on their pottery or their tablets or in their writings?

Heisenberg, W. (1973). Development of concepts in the history of quantum theory. In The physicist's conception of nature (pp. 264-275). Springer, Dordrecht.

315. Do you think if you had the opportunity and had of put your mind to it that you could have been the best at anything you wanted to?

INSIGHTS: Is it just that we aren't feeling something that determines whether we can't accomplish it or not? Are all things actually within our reach, but it is that we aren't really that motivated? Or are things more complex than that?

Wood, A. M., Linley, P. A., Maltby, J., Kashdan, T. B., & Hurling, R. (2011). Using personal and psychological strengths leads to increases in well-being over time: A longitudinal study and the development of the strengths use questionnaire. Personality and Individual Differences, 50(1), 15-19.

316. Why do some parts of the world get rain and some don't?

INSIGHTS: Why do we have deserts? And why are some places all rain and almost no sun? What is it that makes it this way? And if I want sun and no rain, where can I live and where shouldn't I live? Likewise, where are great places to grow crops versus places where I am destined to have my crops fail?

Oki, T., Entekhabi, D., & Harrold, T. I. (1999). The global water cycle. Global energy and water cycles, 10, 27.

317. What do you think needs to be reinvented?

INSIGHTS: Is there anything that needs to be rebuilt from the bottom up? Can you think of anything that needs total disassembly and be redesigned again? If so, what would you say could use a total overhaul?

Pausas, J. G., & Bond, W. J. (2019). Humboldt and the reinvention of nature. Journal of Ecology, 107(3), 1031-1037.

318. What is the best solution to the world garbage problems?

INSIGHTS: What is the best thing we can do to get rid of the world's garbage? Given that the population is likely to reach 10 billion in the not-so-distant future, what are we going to do then?

Dautel, S. L. (2009). Transoceanic trash: international and United States strategies for the great Pacific Garbage Patch. Golden Gate U. Envtl. LJ, 3, 181.

319. Would you rather be born with talent, or work your way into becoming skilled?

INSIGHTS: Would you like to build your own personal empire from the ground up? Or would you like to avoid all the work, pain, and frustration and just walk into it all pre-made just for you? Is it easier to just be lucky in life? And why might this be?

Nadelhoffer, T. (2005). Skill, luck, control, and intentional action. Philosophical Psychology, 18(3), 341-352.

320. Have you ever known someone who was utterly and totally unfit for a job, but was hellbent on getting it through whatever means (cheating on tests, bootlicking, nepotism, cronyism, etc) that was necessary?

INSIGHTS: Why do these institutions proclaim to the public that they are all about selecting only the finest in talent but then keep getting badly busted in cheating scandals and fraud?

McCabe, D. L., Treviño, L. K., & Butterfield, K. D. (2001). Cheating in academic institutions: A decade of research. Ethics &Behavior, 11(3), 219-232.

321. What, in your opinion, is a 'brilliant' person?

INSIGHTS: Sure, people are brilliant, but what does that mean, exactly? What makes us say they are brilliant but not something like intelligent? And what is the difference, exactly? Why do we have this word, and why is it preferable over others?

Cimpian, A., & Leslie, S. J. (2017). The brilliance trap. Scientific American, 317(3), 60-65.

322. Do you think that there could be some eras or periods of history that might have been all made up?

INSIGHTS: Is everything we're taught in history class true? Is it possible, besides just getting one side of the story, that we could just be getting an entirely bogus account of what has happened? Or do you think it's entirely impossible that someone could have just 'made it all up?'

Doležel, L. (1998). Possible worlds of fiction and history. New Literary History, 29(4), 785-809.

323. Do you believe that enough bad times are sure to yield some good ones?

INSIGHTS: There may be a limit on how many adverse events or 'life shocks' one may be able to endure in their life. A research report from New Zealand in 2004 suggested that people can withstand about seven life shocks. Those who had eight or more were significantly more likely to be condemned to poverty.

Sathiyandra, S., & Matangi-Want, M. The 2004 New Zealand living standards survey: what does it signal about the importance of multiple disadvantage?

324. Is competitiveness overrated?

INSIGHTS: So we win that gold medal, but then after the victory feast, we still go home to bed. And then life goes back to normal. So, was all that work really worth it? Or is it all just something we overhyped in our heads?

Houston, J. M., Queen, J. S., Cruz, N., Vlahov, R., & Gosnell, M. (2015). Personality traits and winning: competitiveness, hypercompetitiveness, and Machiavellianism. North American Journal of Psychology, 17(1).

325. Do you believe that governments are actually hiding evidence of UFOs?

INSIGHTS: Professor Stephen Hawking once said something along the lines that it was odd that the government was so good at hiding UFO evidence, given they weren't so great at doing much else. So, with this idea, do you really think they are hiding things?

Heaton, J. B. (2021). Santa Claus, UFOs, and Widespread Voter Fraud: Bayesian Gullibility and Disinformation from a High-Trust Source. Available at SSRN 3804086

326. Is a person's experience of love controllable?

INSIGHTS: Can we just brush it all off when it gets too much momentum? And if not, why not? Why can't we just shut it off like a switch? Or can we, and it's just some of us that can't?

Acevedo, B. P., & Aron, A. (2009). Does a long-term relationship kill romantic love?. Review of General Psychology, 13(1), 59-65.

327. As a guesstimated percentage, what do you think the overall prevalence of insecurity amongst the collective of humanity currently is?

INSIGHTS: Is everyone perfectly confident about everything? If not, why is that? Are they insecure because of external reasons or internal ones?

Orth, U., Robins, R. W., & Roberts, B. W. (2008). Low self-esteem prospectively predicts depression in adolescence and young adulthood. Journal of personality and social psychology, 95(3), 695.

328. Before the events that actually started Christmas, how do you think people celebrated the day that became known as Christmas way before it became what it is now known for? ...and why?

INSIGHTS: Between Neanderthals and us, when exactly did Christmas start? Or did it not start then? And if not, when exactly did it start and why?

Hyde, W. W. (2017). I THE ORIGIN OF CHRISTMAS. In Paganism to Christianity in the Roman Empire (pp. 249-256). University of Pennsylvania Press.

329. Are you someone who can do rollercoaster and "spinning-type" rides without becoming dizzy, nauseous, and discombobulated?

INSIGHTS: Can you handle being centrifuged and swirled about? How long can you stand to do this? And if you can stand it, how do you think you can do this while some others can't?

Furman, J. M., & Whitney, S. L. (2000). Central causes of dizziness. Physical therapy, 80(2), 179-187.

330. Do you ever think we'll make bionic organs that last longer than we do?

INSIGHTS: Is it possible that we will be able to make body parts that will outlast the maximum known human lifespan? And would it be possible that we could do this such that we might extend the maximal lifetime?

Young, S. (2021). The Science and Technology of Growing Young: An Insider's Guide to the Breakthroughs that Will Dramatically Extend Our Lifespan... and What You Can Do Right Now. BenBella Books.

331. Is artificial intelligence a blessing or a curse?

INSIGHTS: Is AI going to be our ever-faithful servant? Is it always going to work only in the best interests of humans? Or is there a chance of Skynet happening? Also, what about all the jobs it might replace?

Helbing, D. (2019). Machine Intelligence: Blessing or Curse? It Depends on Us! In Towards Digital Enlightenment (pp. 25-39). Springer, Cham.

332. Are some people simply greedy by their nature?

INSIGHTS: Is greed something that is embedded in one's genome and can't be helped? Or is this just a learned trait? Why do some people seem to be more overtaken by greed than others?

Lee, K., & Ashton, M. C. (2013). The H factor of personality: Why some people are manipulative, self-entitled, materialistic, and exploitive—and why it matters for everyone.

333. Do deities need to follow logic to exist?

INSIGHTS: Is there a limit on logic? Is the great test of the universe to see if we can push off all logic and realize that the answer is actually in the illogical? Or do deities follow logic just fine? What is it that we are exactly missing with the great mystery?

Paulos, J. A. (2008). Irreligion: A mathematician explains why the arguments for God just don't add up.

334. Where and when did the idea of the soul come from?

INSIGHTS: If the soul isn't real, then it is an idea. But where exactly did this idea come from, and who was the first to think it up? And perhaps most importantly, why did someone think it up in the first place? Or is this a real thing?

Frede, D., & Reis, B. (Eds.). (2009). Body and soul in ancient philosophy. Walter de Gruyter.

335. Why do all animals and even bacteria run on glucose?

INSIGHTS: Why, oh why, do bacteria and humans both run on glucose? If we are so different and don't share a common ancestor, then why is it that we both use the same fuel? And given that one often can be bad for the other, why would life have us chasing after the same goal?

Fothergill-Gilmore, L. A., & Michels, P. A. (1993). Evolution of glycolysis. Progress in biophysics and molecular biology, 59(2), 105-235.

336. Is going with the flow always the best strategy?

INSIGHTS: Just cause everyone else is doing it, is it logical and smart to follow? Why would going with the flow be the best thing to do? Or is it not always the best thing to do? Why do so many follow others even if it isn't a good plan?

Leroy, S., Shipp, A. J., Blount, S., & Licht, J. G. (2015). Synchrony preference: Why some people go with the flow and some don't. Personnel Psychology, 68(4), 759-809.

337. Is social superiority/inferiority hardwired in the human brain?

INSIGHTS: Why does social hierarchy exist? Why do we need some to be or to think they are above others? What purpose does this serve? Or does it serve any purpose at all? What is it that may potentially compel some people to place themselves above others?

Zink, C. F., Tong, Y., Chen, Q., Bassett, D. S., Stein, J. L., & Meyer-Lindenberg, A. (2008). Know your place: neural processing of social hierarchy in humans. Neuron, 58(2), 273-283.

338. Should we sequence the DNA of museum specimens of extinct animals?

INSIGHTS: Since we have museums, why don't we take a bit of a sample from some of the specimens on hand and sequence their DNA? What would be wrong with this idea?

Brunson, K., & Reich, D. (2019). The promise of paleogenomics beyond our own species. Trends in Genetics, 35(5), 319-329.

339. Do you have what it takes to complete an Arctic or Antarctic expedition?

INSIGHTS: Could you stand the freezing temperatures and other hardships that come along with an Arctic or Antarctic expedition? Could you deal with the constant cold weather and the potentials for complete disaster that would accompany such a journey?

Guly, H. R. (2012). Snow blindness and other eye problems during the heroic age of Antarctic exploration. Wilderness & environmental medicine, 23(1), 77-82.

340. Do things like cells or transistors add up to become something more?

INSIGHTS: When we put together a complex network of simple components, is it possible to end up with something that acts nothing like the things it is composed of? Our experience seems to suggest so, but why does this happen? What makes this sort of thing 'occur?'

Aziz-Alaoui, M., & Bertelle, C. (Eds.). (2009). From system complexity to emergent properties. Springer Science & Business Media.

341. Is it possible that a population could become too dense and therefore affect human social behavior?

INSIGHTS: Does the density of a population affect its mindset? Does living in crammed conditions have an effect on people? Or do people just make more out of it than there really is? In terms of being packed together, how much is too much?

Calhoun, J. B. (1962). Population density and social pathology. Scientific American, 206(2), 139-149.

342. How long do you think a closed, self-contained colony on Mars would last?

INSIGHTS: So a bunch of people head out to Mars where there is a great big living quarters and station. Over time, they begin to populate. So what would happen then if people began to populate Mars but didn't have a way of expanding their living quarters? Would it all work out okay?

Calhoun, J. B. (1973). Death squared: the explosive growth and demise of a mouse population.

343. Are you accountable for your own actions?

INSIGHTS: Are all the things you do completely under your total control? Do you really have control over the muscle spasm? Do you have control over that accidental slip when trying hard not to pass gas? Just how much control do we really have over ourselves?

Alper, J. S., & Beckwith, J. (1993). Genetic fatalism and social policy: the implications of behavior genetics research. The Yale journal of biology and medicine, 66(6), 511.

344. Do you believe that objects can be possessed/haunted?

INSIGHTS: Is there a little bit of ghost in everything? If so, how do you know so? What would make you think inanimate objects would have some living element to them? What would make you think that something could actually be haunted?

Goff, P. (2017). Panpsychism. The Blackwell Companion to Consciousness, 106-124.

345. How would you give an AI motivation?

INSIGHTS: Humans have motivation. Mice have motivation. Even bacteria have motivation. But, for an AI to 'come to life,' one thing it might need is motivation. But how would one be able to craft an AI such that it would have certain motivations?

O'Reilly, R. C. (2020). Unraveling the mysteries of motivation. Trends in cognitive sciences, 24(6), 425-434.

346. For those of you concerned with climate change, how well do you understand the five mass extinction events?

INSIGHTS: Extinctions are not a new thing. Earth has had five major extinctions so far and likely isn't finished. So, what dictates what survives and what doesn't?

McElwain, J. C., & Punyasena, S. W. (2007). Mass extinction events and the plant fossil record. Trends in ecology & evolution, 22(10), 548-557.

347. Are we all equal in potential?

INSIGHTS: Can I do the same things that you can do just as well as you can? Or are each of us specialized in our own strengths? Or more so, are only some of us capable while others may not be? How can we tell for sure what the answer is?

Guo, G., & Stearns, E. (2002). The social influences on the realization of genetic potential for intellectual development. Social forces, 80(3), 881-910.

348. What is the future for power generation?

INSIGHTS: Can we just keep doing what we are doing and be fine for power generation indefinitely? Or do we need a new method and/or a new fuel? How might we be able to do this?

Ünak, T. (2000). What is the potential use of thorium in the future energy production technology?. Progress in nuclear energy, 37(1-4), 137-144.

349. Do you think working from home should be a regular thing from now on?

INSIGHTS: Is it always a great idea to have everyone crowding the highways and roads so early in the morning and then again around dinner time? Is this the only way business can be run? Is there anything else, or is working from home just some kind of impossibility for some reason or another?

Dockery, M., & Bawa, S. (2020). Working from Home in the COVID-19 Lockdown. BCEC, 19, 1-5.

350. Why can't we bring people back from the dead?

INSIGHTS: So what is the exact problem as to why we can't revive someone from the dead? What is so far gone that there is no hope of ever reviving them? And if something is too far gone, at what point did it hit the point of no return?

Galloway, A., Birkby, W. H., Jones, A. M., Henry, T. E., & Parks, B. O. (1989). Decay rates of human remains in an arid environment. Journal of Forensic Science, 34(3), 607-616.

351. Could we be getting spied on?

INSIGHTS: Is your cell phone really off, or did someone hack the camera and now, despite being off, is able to watch your every move? Or did they hack the microphone? And are they able to listen in on you? Is all this possible?

Kröger, J. L., & Raschke, P. (2019, July). Is my phone listening in? On the feasibility and detectability of mobile eavesdropping. In IFIP Annual Conference on Data and Applications Security and Privacy (pp. 102-120). Springer, Cham.

352. How many of the world's problems are due to not being united?

INSIGHTS: Does our division help us? Does it help to be broken up into groups of 'us and them?' Is that really the best way to live life? Is there really so much difference between us all that we have to be divided?

Aumer-Ryan, K., & Hatfield, E. C. (2007). The design of everyday hate: A qualitative and quantitative analysis. Interpersona: An International Journal on Personal Relationships, 1(2), 143-172.

353. Is kindness a normal behavior?

INSIGHTS: Is it a normal thing to be kind? Or is it a normal thing for humans to actually be hostile towards one another? Or indifferent? What is the default setting, and what is the exception? Is everyone in the world nice? Are most people nice? Or do they seem like they have other things to do?

Phillips, A., & Taylor, B. (2009). On kindness. Macmillan.

354. How often do you think anger is used as a distraction?

INSIGHTS: Do people just get angry cause they feel that way? Or do people get angry cause they know it might be helpful to avoid something they don't want to deal with by being angry?

Pratkanis, A. R. (2007). Social influence analysis: An index of tactics.

355. Do you think that we will ever fully map out the universe in terms of elementary particles and the forces between them?

INSIGHTS: Will we be able to determine all the fundamental particles in the universe? Or will we have to evolve into the next step, or even more, in order to be able to comprehend what's really at the heart of it all?

Cabaret, D. M., Grandou, T., Grange, G. M., & Perrier, E. (2021). Elementary Particles: What are they? Substances, elements and primary matter. arXiv preprint arXiv:2103.05522.

356. Do you think String Theory will eventually lead to figuring out the universe?

INSIGHTS: Is string theory the way? Or did these guys just not hear Godel? Will it bring us to the answers? Or at least closer to them?

Gubser, S. S. (2010). The little book of string theory. Princeton University Press.

Berto, F. (2011). There's something about Gödel: the complete guide to the incompleteness theorem. John Wiley & Sons.

357. Why can't we live forever?

INSIGHTS: Why do we have a fixed lifespan? What is it in the universe that has us existing in such a short time span? Why can't we just exist forever? What would it take for us to be able to exist forever?

Rando, T. A. (2006). Stem cells, ageing and the quest for immortality. Nature, 441(7097), 1080-1086.

358. When did humans begin to take stories and/or narratives as beliefs?

INSIGHTS: Once campfire stories began, at what point after did stories become opulent enough that they began to be taken as beliefs? Or is this not the case? What else could be the case if this was not the case?

Witzel, E. M. (2012). The origins of the world's mythologies. Oxford University Press.

359. Are people generally clear on where to place blame?

INSIGHTS: Are people so sure that they know where blame exactly belongs? Are they perfectly sure they know who and/or what is really at fault? When something goes wrong, is it always just one thing that did it? Or is it a number of things? Or was it something that happened long before it?

Douglas, M. (2013). Risk and blame. Routledge.

360. Have different generations experienced different childhoods?

INSIGHTS: Is every childhood the same? Did the kids growing up in the medieval Black Death times have the same childhood as the kids that grew up in the 1980s? Is it all really just the same? Or do external conditions have a lot, if not all, to do with the quality of a childhood?

Campbell, W. K., Campbell, S. M., Siedor, L. E., & Twenge, J. M. (2015). Generational differences are real and useful. Industrial and Organizational Psychology, 8(3), 324-331.

361. Will our freedoms increase as the world population increases?

INSIGHTS: With more people to control, will we all end up with more freedom individually, overall? Or will we end up with a bunch of conformers? Will authorities be limited in their power? Or will they be able to devise ways of making us more compliant? And then, moving beyond authorities, does the environment itself have its own limits to our freedoms?

St'ahel, R. (2016). Environmental limits of personal freedom. PHILOSOPHICA, 2, 1.

362. Is modern science run in the best way possible?

INSIGHTS: Is the way science is currently done the best possible way it can be done? Is the whole system fool-proof and fraud-proof? Or are there some holes in the system that need addressing?

Schekman, R. (2013). How journals like Nature, Cell and Science are damaging science. The Guardian, 9, 12.

363. Would you rather one single world government?

INSIGHTS: Would it just be easier if there was just one single government rather than all the governments that there are, plus all the subdivisions that branch off from them? Is this a feasible solution for all people? Or is it better if we keep the system we are using right now?

Zolo, D. (2013). Cosmopolis: prospects for world government. John Wiley & Sons.

364. Do you think the world could exist without police?

INSIGHTS: Do you really think we need police? Would humans really conduct their behavior in benevolent ways in the absence of police? Would it work just fine when there is a massive traffic accident to just have all involved parties sort it out? Could it work?

McDowell, M. G., & Fernandez, L. A. (2018). 'Disband, Disempower, and Disarm': Amplifying the theory and practice of police abolition. Critical Criminology, 26(3), 373-391.

365. What is the percentage of fraudulent scientific publications?

INSIGHTS: Is science completely innocent once things move from the bench and into the office? Would anyone ever write anything fraudulent in something as important as a scientific publication? Has it ever been done before? Why?

Foo, J. Y. A., & Tan, X. J. A. (2014). Analysis and implications of retraction period and coauthorship of fraudulent publications. Accountability in research, 21(3), 198-210.

366. Is social media bad for mental health?

INSIGHTS: Is social media a positive, a negative, or does it have no effect on its users? With conversation being a bit different than in person, what might this do over a long period of time to a given individual? Is there an effect? If not, why not?

Berryman, C., Ferguson, C. J., & Negy, C. (2018). Social media use and mental health among young adults. Psychiatric quarterly, 89(2), 307-314.

367. Do you think most people can admit when they are wrong?

INSIGHTS: Is it a common trait that you see in most people to be able to admit when they are wrong? Or do most of the people in your sphere of influence cling to their position with unwavering stubbornness? What is the more common move? And most importantly, why is this?

Savion, L. (2009). Clinging to Discredited Beliefs: The Larger Cognitive Story. Journal of the Scholarship of Teaching and Learning, 9(1), 81-92.

368. What is life?

INSIGHTS: What is life, really? Why do we exist, and for what reason? What is this whole thing that is called life? Why did it happen at all, and why does it keep happening?

Margulis, L., & Sagan, D. (2000). What is life? Univ of California Press.

369. Can Marxism work?

INSIGHTS: Could H. sapiens be capable of making and following a system where there is no one who goes without a home and no one who goes without eating a meal? Could we be the creature to pull something like this off? Or does H. sapiens go along better with a capitalist system? If so, why? And why can't humans do a Marxist-type system?

Ruccio, D. F. (1992). Failure of socialism, future of socialists? Rethinking Marxism, 5(2), 6-22.

370. Physical, mental or emotional, do you consider yourself a fighter?

INSIGHTS: Do you think fighting is a waste of time or something that should be avoided at all costs? Or do you consider yourself someone who is ready to flip the table at the slightest sound of an insulting remark?

Milton, M. (2004). Being a Fighter. Existential Analysis: Journal of the Society for Existential Analysis, 15(1).

371. Why is science denial and flat-earth theory so popular?

INSIGHTS: What is so popular about denying reality? Even if you don't like it and don't want to hear it, can you prove that it isn't the reality? Claims are just claims till proven otherwise. Until then, they are just claims. So where is the proof for all the other 'ideas' if no one likes what science says?

McIntyre, L. (2021). How to Talk to a Science Denier: Conversations with Flat Earthers, Climate Deniers, and Others Who Defy Reason. MIT Press.

372. Do narcissists prefer Twitter or Facebook?

INSIGHTS: Which platform is better for narcissists? Which one and why? Most especially, why would narcissists have a preference? Which one is more advantageous to the narcissistic personality?

Davenport, S. W., Bergman, S. M., Bergman, J. Z., & Fearrington, M. E. (2014). Twitter versus Facebook: Exploring the role of narcissism in the motives and usage of different social media platforms. Computers in Human Behavior, 32, 212-220.

373. Why does Facebook stay afloat?

INSIGHTS: Everyone says they hate Facebook, but then, sure as sure gets, there they are, posting away their newest photos of their cat, Bubbles, on Facebook. So, if the platform is resented so much, what keeps people so hooked?

Alloway, T., Runac, R., Quershi, M., & Kemp, G. (2014). Is Facebook linked to selfishness? Investigating the relationships among social media use, empathy, and narcissism. Social Networking, 2014.

374. What is the evolutionary basis for bullying?

INSIGHTS: More than a million times, bullying has been labeled as toxic and destructive, yet, here we are, still full of bullies and their victims. So, despite all the activism towards ending bullying, why do we see it still happening, despite all the push that goes against it?

Kaburu, S. S., Inoue, S., & NEWTON-FISHER, N. E. (2013). Death of the alpha: Within-community lethal violence among chimpanzees of the Mahale Mountains National Park. American journal of primatology, 75(8), 789-797.

375. Why do people get tattoos?

INSIGHTS: Given that humans have been modifying their bodies for some time, is it just a quick fad to get tattoos? Or is there more to this practice than is first assumed? Or is this just all a way to find some sort of personal distinction in a hyperpopulated world?

Kang, M., & Jones, K. (2007). Why do people get tattoos? Contexts, 6(1), 42-47.

376. Why do people join groups?

INSIGHTS: Why does so much of humanity tend towards being part of some group? Why aren't we just stepping off as individuals and going our own way? What is it about humans and being a part of a group?

Hogg, M. A., Hohman, Z. P., & Rivera, J. E. (2008). Why do people join groups? Three motivational accounts from social psychology. Social and Personality Psychology Compass, 2(3), 1269-1280.

377. Do animals have personalities?

INSIGHTS: Is your dog an optimist? Is your cat a reserved pessimist? Or is your friend's pet iguana a narcissist? Do animals have their own distinct personalities? Or are we imposing our perception of them upon them?

Wolf, M., Van Doorn, G. S., Leimar, O., & Weissing, F. J. (2007). Life-history trade-offs favour the evolution of animal personalities. Nature, 447(7144), 581-584.

378. Is there such a thing as the true self?

INSIGHTS: So we all know ourselves, right? It's us, just us; we are the 'us.' Or is the actual case a lot more complex than all this? Is it true that we are who we think we are? Or is there more to our true selves than we commonly assume?

Sparby, T., Edelhäuser, F., & Weger, U. W. (2019). The True Self. Critique, Nature, and Method. Frontiers in psychology, 10, 2250.

380. Do people need ideology?

INSIGHTS: Although it seems that the powers that be insist that the people have an ideology, is it entirely true that people absolutely need it?

Mannheim, K. (2013). Ideology and utopia. Routledge.

379. Does astrology actually work?

INSIGHTS: Is there any truth to astrology? Or is it just some form of pseudoscience? Or is it that there is magic to it, and it does work? Or, is there some other force at work that ends up giving us valid conclusions? Or is this just all some form of bias?

Allum, N. (2011). What makes some people think astrology is scientific? Science Communication, 33(3), 341-366.

381. Do you know how an internal combustion engine works?

INSIGHTS: We use them everyday. They are all around us. In fact, they keep our world in motion. But do we know exactly how such a common item exactly works? Do you know how the engine does what it does?

Gupta, H. N. (2012). Fundamentals of internal combustion engines. PHI Learning Pvt. Ltd.

382. Do you understand Einstein's Special Theory of Relativity?

INSIGHTS: We hear it all the time on science documentaries and other TV programming, but do most people have a good idea of this theory and how it was composed? Given that it is so widely talked about, one has to wonder if everyone is clear on this theory?

French, A. P. (2017). Special relativity. CRC Press.

383. What is an intellectual?

INSIGHTS: What is an actual intellectual? As with all familiar but slightly mysterious terms, do we know where the line is exactly drawn between intellectual and 'the others?'

Ritchhart, R. (2002). Intellectual character: What it is, why it matters, and how to get it. John Wiley & Sons.

384. Why has it become fashionable to shun obvious intelligence and verifiable knowledge?

INSIGHTS: Why would it be popular to spread nonsense? Why would people go through such extreme efforts to push the idea that there is a flat earth, despite it being long proven otherwise? What is it that is making people turn away from the blatantly obvious?

Merkley, E. (2020). Anti-intellectualism, populism, and motivated resistance to expert consensus. Public Opinion Quarterly, 84(1), 24-48.

385. What determines how your life goes?

INSIGHTS: Is it all my choices that prevail in life? Or does the external world have a say? And more so, do others have a say in how my life goes? And if not, do their decisions affect me at all? Or are we unaffected by the choices and actions of others?

Bandura, A. (1982). The psychology of chance encounters and life paths. American psychologist, 37(7), 747.

386. Is favoritism the major driver behind advancement in workplaces and organizations?

INSIGHTS: Does everyone equally and always get hired and advanced based on their hard work alone? Or do people advance and get hired because they are liked? Could it be that one force dominates the other? Or are they even? Or are they not the case?

Bramoullé, Y., & Goyal, S. (2009). Favoritism.

387. Does Cancel Culture actually exist?

INSIGHTS: Does cancel culture really exist? Many of its proponents state that it is just justice being delivered where it is needed. But it is one thing for the social justice warriors to point out injustices, but what about companies that back these 'rulings?' Could this be the canceling by the culture?

Norris, P. (2021). Cancel Culture: Myth or Reality? Political Studies, 00323217211037023.

388. What is the point of middlemen in the business world?

INSIGHTS: Are middlemen needed by other men in business? Or is it that middlemen are needed by other middlemen? What is it that these people do in the business world? What is their role, and do you exactly know what it is?

Biglaiser, G. (1993). Middlemen as experts. The RAND journal of Economics, 212-223.

389. How many people could be real psychopaths?

INSIGHTS: Although the statistics might say this or say that, how many people are actually born such that they have this affliction? Of course, many of us are quick to label those whom we see as being heartless a psychopath, but, what are the real numbers?

Coid, J., Yang, M., Ullrich, S., Roberts, A., & Hare, R. D. (2009). Prevalence and correlates of psychopathic traits in the household population of Great Britain. International journal of law and psychiatry, 32(2), 65-73.

390. What do you think is the cause of existential crisis being so common?

INSIGHTS: Why does it seem like humanity is having a giant existential crisis, or is this just the way it has always been? Is it just that this happens to all people at some point in their lives and that now, because of the internet, we hear about it more? Or is it that contemporary times are bringing it out more in people?

Andrews, M. (2016). The existential crisis. Behavioral development bulletin, 21(1), 104.

391. Do you wish to leave a legacy?

INSIGHTS: Are you out to leave your mark in the great book of humanity? Are you looking to create or achieve something much greater than even you can imagine? What is it that you wish to achieve? Or do you wish to remain obscure and enjoy your life and the time you have to yourself?

Sligte, D. J., Nijstad, B. A., & De Dreu, C. K. (2013). Leaving a legacy neutralizes negative effects of death anxiety on creativity. Personality and Social Psychology Bulletin, 39(9), 1152-1163.

392. Do I actually know what I really want?

INSIGHTS: I want a coffee. But then I gotta wonder, do I? Do I really want that coffee, or am I living such that I am on autopilot?

Byrne, A. (2011). Knowing what I want.

393. In general, what is the thing you would say that people talk about the most?

INSIGHTS: What is it that most people talk about? Do they talk about science? And do they do this constantly? Or do people talk about fun and leisure? Or is it something else completely?

Dunbar, R. I. (2004). Gossip in evolutionary perspective. Review of general psychology, 8(2), 100-110.

394. Is time real?

INSIGHTS: Are we just making up something out of nothing based on our instincts and innate notions? Is our head confusing us and making up a dimension that actually doesn't exist in objective reality?

Ingthorsson, R. (1998). McTaggart and the Unreality of Time. Axiomathes, 9(3).

395. How does time work, exactly?

INSIGHTS: Time is just more than a clock, right? But what is it, and how does it work? What is it about time that seems so puzzling? How does it work?

Stoneham, T. (2009). Time and truth: the presentism-eternalism debate. Philosophy, 84(2), 201-218.

396. Are time and space apart from the human mind?

INSIGHTS: Are we in the same 'thing?' Or is our mind separate from the universe? If so, how do we know this, and who was the one that proved it conclusively?

Fine, K. (2002). The question of realism. In Individuals, Essence and Identity (pp. 3-48). Springer, Dordrecht.

397. Why do humans form beliefs?

INSIGHTS: Do we really need to believe anything? A quick thought might suggest to us that there is merit in having beliefs, especially when time is a factor. But, when we have time to spare, do we really need beliefs?

Eller, J. D. (2014). Introducing anthropology of religion: culture to the ultimate. Routledge.

398. Are you familiar with 'Occam's Razor?'

INSIGHTS: Is this a shaving device? Of course, this type of razor is designed to shave off a sort of noise. But how does it do this, and how effective is it? Most importantly, how can it be used?

Gibbs, P., & Hiroshi, S. (1996). What is Occam's razor.

399. How will the universe end?

INSIGHTS: If the universe began, then is it safe to assume it will end? Many are convinced this is the case, and not by guessing either. The question is, when will it end, and how will it end?

Bahr, B., Lemmer, B., & Piccolo, R. (2016). The end of the universe. In Quirky Quarks (pp. 314-319). Springer, Berlin, Heidelberg.

400. What happened before the Big Bang?

INSIGHTS: Did the universe happen with no cause? Did it just come into existence from nothing at all? Can we take this to be true? Can something come from nothing? If so, how so?

Bojowald, M. (2007). What happened before the Big Bang? Nature Physics, 3(8), 523-525.

ACKNOWLEDGMENTS

The following people and/or Twitter accounts were an inspiration for this title:

Michelle Garcia, @Latina_Schatje; Dmitry, @dmitryro; Nigama RV, @NigamaRv; R.M. Olson, @richolsonwriter; Clayton Taylor Wood, @ClaytonTWood; *Sassy Savvy Adventurer*, @SassysavvyLia; no worries, @no1worries1; Patricia Taylor Wells, @patwellstx; Hap Hapner, @HapHapner; El Espléndido Señor Jackalicious™, @JackalishScott; She_Persisted, @Impeach_Cheeto; Fiona Murden, @FionaMurden; Jeffery Brown, @WhyIteachtoday; Nika Kabiri, JD PhD, @nikakabiri; Chris Toepker, @GoProFun; Dan Sihota, @DanSihota; Daniel Sumner, @DanielS20852473; Jeff Crowder, @_megz__, M.Carraway; Victoria Marswell, @vicmarswell; Mali X Sensei, @iammalicool; Bradley Simpson, @orcish_dreams; @JeffCrowder16; Kathy Forough, @kforough1; Pasithea Chan, @PasitheaChan; Jonblair Books, @JonblairB; Alyssa, @AlyssaGoodwitch; Eadbhárd Ó Corraidhín, @Readwhenstoned; Dr. Victoria Rose, @VictoriaRosePhD; Mishka, @__poetism; Cherry, @CherryWrites; Nicole, @nicolep79mia; @Alpha_Lupus; Dave Evans, @CCWorkfloor; John Brage, @JBrage67; Jim Hamilton, @Chaosity8; Steve Naisbitt, @naisbitt_steve; Jeff Kalac, @JeffKalac; Pamela, @PamelaStaton5; Anthony Beaulne, @anthony_beaulne; Emae Church, @EmaeChurch; ThePragmatist, @ThePragmatist5; David Padilla, @d_ast777; Janie, @INTProbably; Richard Bacula, @RichardBacula; Scott Bell, @Scottslifeeh; ObviousMan, @Solarman1955; Bence Tóth, @BenceTt33734272; E.R Clouston, @e_r_clouston; Charles Flowers LMT, @Str8EdgeMarine; Eugene Galt, @eugene_galt; Derek Prowse, @Derek_Prowse; GL Francis, @merelecroix; J. W. Traphagan, @john_traphagan; Ivet Putnam, @PutnamIvet; WriteEthan, @WriteEthan; Katy B Sweet, @KatyBSweet1; Tina Hartigan™, @TinaHartigan1; commandergirl, @illyrian598; C.E. Steiger, @CurtSteiger; @FireTigerGirl; Pat Scaramuzza, @genocideman; Peggy Harkins, @PeggyHarkins; Shelley, @ShambhalaReign; The Lyran Empress, @LyranEmpress; Reed Alexander, @ReedsHorror; Michael, @Mikethewander1; SedonaCAuthor, @SedonaCAuthor; Andrew Slinde, @AndrewSlinde; Thomas

Muriuki, @klenstert; Sean Newberg, @newberg_sean; Lovely Lance Lumley, @lovelylance1; Matthew Arnold Stern, @maswriter; @wstevewilson; D. H. Kaye, @DHKaye3; Uneasy Writer, @HorrorAwaits; Todd Vercoe, @ToddVercoe; Stephanie, @STEPHANIE_DLCG; Jim, @hansonji; Dr. Deb Collins-Lindh, EdD, @DebraLindh; Thomas Eric Hill, @Thomas4192; B Harrison Smith, @HarrisonSmith85; Ava Banton, @AvaBanton; Thomas, @ThomasTheUnwise; András Zöld, @AndrasZold; Clinton A. Love, @AuthorOfGehenna; D.G. Wright, @BooksUndCoffee; Sara Snarkapuss, @SSnarkapuss; @igornamus; Cassie, @Cassie04084401; Angie Shaffer, @write_the_grey; Daniel Forbes, @DanielsTales; morganalways, @teresam2356; Pat Maxwell, @Swisher3333; DNT, @letweetsfromd; 𝕾.𝕵.𝕽.3 (𝕾𝔱𝔢𝔳𝔢𝔫 𝕽.), @therealSIR3; Graciela L, @Graciela32; Murphalupagus, @mybigcity; Michael Beyer, @mbeyer51; Essence Rayne, @rayne_essence; Ryan, @Ryan_Daigler; @jdf1188; Ghosthorse Dentist, @GhostHDentist; Paul Reeves, @Paul_A_Reeves; S. Goodey, @goodeywrites; joannmay, @joannmay91; Kerry Creech, @CreechKerry; Damian Harpel, @DamianGHarpel; VoxVorago, @VoxVorago; Mick, @MrMick2021; Nora Pattugalam, @norap_author; ReubenSalsa, @SalsaReuben; Flippant Interjectionist, @DanSanderson10; HrH. Rev. Dr. Garnet Smuczer, NaD AMPAD, @Garnet_Smuczer; Lyle Closs, @lylecloss; MaryContrary, @contrarymary197; Ripusudan Srivastava, @RipusudanSriva2; Grow with Clint, @Grow_With_Clint; Sharon De Pontes, @SharonDepontes; Chad Zaugg, @ChadZaugg; Linda Douglas, @LindaMDouglas; thurayya Candle, @thurayya888; Judy Ramsook, @JudyRamsook; james dusenbᴇʀᴄʜ, @JamesDusenbery. Pᴇɳɳɥ Eʟɑυɲᴇ, @NCG1rl; Maureen Twomey, @Maureen_2me; Lisa, @ReidyCarrick; Alexa Sommers, @AlexaSommers; becka russo, @beckarusso; georgewyoung, @georgewyounggm1; p.m.terrell, @pmterrell; slbutlerauthor, @slbutlerauthor; Daniel Paice, @DanJWrites; Jaggz, @JaggzNasty; @LeastRoad; @WritingsFromJen; Bryan Matthews, @BryanMatthews23; Doug Brower, @DougBrower7; Valerie, @catonashland; The Great and Powerful Fexo, @TheFexo; *The Rebourne Identity*, @RebourneThe; Jenn Leah, @Jenn_Leah13; marie france revelin, @abdeline; danpliszka,

@danpliszka; bookmanwhb@gmail.com, @bookmanwhb13; @sdballentine; Ned Stephenson, @stephenson_ned; Nancy-Maxxed Out-Botwin, @RealNancyBotwin; Richard LeDue, @LedueRichard; Hillbilly Highlander, @HillbillyHigh11; Sydney Alexis Phillips, @SydMarketsStuff; Tim Heffernan, @Heff61; Michelle Beauchamp, Ph.D., @MichellesRedux; Arthur Mitchell, @MitchMars; R Welkin, Galactic thinkers fascinate me, CANADIAN, @SfWelkin; Cricket of Good Fortune™, C.S. Kjar, @cskjar; @LuckyCricket8; The Frogtown Croaker, @frogtowncroaker; A J King, @ThisAJKing; Dorks, Dogs & Dingos, @dorksdogsdingos; Victoria Jane, @JaneJannievic; darkpassenger, @invisibleagent2; Mohammed Mizan, @rmmmizan; Raegun Sparks, @SparksRaegun; Tyra, @TyraLynn369; Shari Chadderdon, @ShariChadderdon; Thom Forr, @2byIV; @lisaN4kids; Elizabeth Merck, @ElizabethMerck; cutigs, @cutigs1; Sandra Howard, @ziggyzagzag; Katrina R. Lippolis, @kitkatpoetess; Cycle Forward Films, @CycleForward; Paul Bccp, @paulbccp; @RobertBHayek; Mj Pettengill, @Mj_Pettengill; Susan Hubchak, @hubchak; @LeslieDRush; Miranda Moeller, @miranda_moeller; Stephan B., @StephanRBarnard; Ensa Conteh, @conteh_ensa; Mary Catherine La Mar, @LaMarchinaMC; Tipsy Versus Everything, @TipsyVersus; Peggy Sue Perry, @ghostwriter4God; Shah Ali Riyad, @ShahTheWanderer; Adamlikesbbq, @Adam12332871709; Elizabeth Merck, @ElizabethMerck; LinneaAroldMichel, @LinneaMichel; Cari, @CariLynn_01; Lisa Ann, @LisaAnn96B; Anonymous, @sincerelystaid; Pamela Kaval, @KavalAuthorActs; Rosie O'Linguist, @cassellrose77; E. Lynn Cormick, @ELynnCormick; 𝕱𝖔𝖗𝖊𝖛𝖊𝖗𝖘𝖎𝖓𝖓𝖊𝖗86, @Foreversinner11; snow leopard, @southpawsnowcat; Barney Blather, @BarneyBlather; Lauren Ipsome, @LaurenIpsome; Model_kindness, @Model_kindness; Wendy Waters, @wa_waters; Mona Tea O'Henry, @monaohenry; Novyl, @lyv0n; @BelaWolf; Girl Under The Dome, @girl_dome; AndyPopeInTheWoods, @AndyPopeInTheW1; Mellow Demon, @Mell0wDem0n; Mark Gelinas, @Elderac; Hollie E. Townsend, @HollieETownsend; amrita, @84amrita; lnicol10252aol.com, @lnicol10252aolc; Krisa, @NeonKrisa; Mary Elizabeth, @meromoser67; Lynn Morgan Rosser,

@LynnMRosser; muhammad Andre Fauzi, @MuhammadAndreF2; Steve, @shortcomment2; Little J, @hamilpufftweets; jupiter.magna, @JupiterMagna; Unholy Jim, @jimmclou; Dolly Israni, @ddollified; @YUKOWAS; Michael Soltis, @MikeySoltis; Fully Kimmunized, @vinekimber; Frankie Waters, @FrankieWatersEd; ze_Cat, @Poker_Spaz; FJDib, @fj_dib; Dona, @natollaed; R*K*_*, @robinkoretsky; Judy Ford, @JudyFordAuthor; Tasha s, @PcflWtrs; J.E. Clarke, @JEClarke4; Michael Ribeiro, @RealMichaelRib; Fran, @frankflores111; Donna, @DonnaAd17752818; Ron Sweet, @RadioRonIsOnAir; Clifford Smith, @clifford4five6; Black Flames, @Freddie_blacks; Lin, @LibrarylinM; Lisa Ann, @LisaAnn96B; Andrea Petitte, @AndreaPWriter; Iva Ogletree, @OgletreeIva; TashInTheClouds, @TashPoetry; Robert Cain, @bobcain45; J. A. Martin, @Ghostsofthe812; DeDe Ramey, @RameyDede;

To those whom I might have missed here, please forgive me!

269

Made in United States
Troutdale, OR
07/31/2023

11707857R00156